D1165367

NSIDE PUBLIC LIBRARY

3 1232 00498 3369

...dered
...t. It is not
...ted the Nihil
...gree with the
...tements expressed.

POEMS OF
St THÉRÈSE OF LISIEUX

———

Translated by

ALAN BANCROFT

Fount
An Imprint of HarperCollinsPublishers

HarperCollins*Publishers*,
77–85 Fulham Palace Road
Hammersmith, London W6 8JB

First published in Great Britain
in 1996 by HarperCollins*Publishers*

1 3 5 7 9 10 8 6 4 2

© in the translation, introduction and original notes
Alan Bancroft 1996

Alan Bancroft asserts the moral right to be
identified as the translator of these poems,
the author of the introduction and the
compiler of the notes

A catalogue record for this book is
available from the British Library

ISBN 0 00 627950 3

Printed and bound in Great Britain by
Caledonian International Book Manufacturing Ltd, Glasgow, G64

The translator dedicates
this book, with gratitude, to
Father John A. Feeley

FOREWORD

by Very Reverend Canon Francis J. Ripley

———————

It is with very special pleasure that I respond to Alan Bancroft's invitation to contribute a foreword to his translation of poems of St Thérèse of Lisieux. I must have been in my early teens when Thérèse first captured me. Towards the end of my Daily Missal I discovered her 'Offering of herself as a holocaust to God's Merciful Love'. I read it and was immediately gripped, captivated by it. From then on I recited it every day after receiving Holy Communion. Love of that prayer led me to enquire about its writer. So I read Thérèse's autobiography. That impressed me more than any other book I had read.

If Thérèse captured me, as I believe she did, my pursuit of her became one of the dominant elements in my spiritual life. Throughout my student days I read everything I could find about her. A high spot came when Monsignor Vernon Johnson invited me to one of his retreats in Lisieux. I was one of the foundation members of the Association of Priests of Saint Thérèse of the Child Jesus and until his death I maintained a close friendship with Monsignor Johnson.

Thérèse has always guided me, often in quite delicate ways, and I can well recall the guidance having involved, specifically, that same great prayer by which she had captured me as a boy of twelve at school. When I read Alan Bancroft's translation of her poems I experienced a sensation rather like the one I remember when reading the Act of Offering for the first time. The spirit of St Thérèse is all concentrated in that offering of herself as a victim of love which she wrote out and put in the book of the Gospels she always carried around with her, close to her heart. There it was found after her death.

Thérèse's devotion was not only to God's love but to His *merciful* love. The new *Catechism of the Catholic Church* has six quotations from her writings, more than from any of her Saint-sisters. One of the quotations is from her Act of Offering to Merciful Love. In it she says 'I do not wish to amass merits for heaven, I wish to work for Your love alone':

> This rose, *un-petaled now*,
>   is, Holy Child! that heart
>   (The figure's true)
>   Which wants to immolate
>   itself – in every part
>   Always, for You.
>   (Poem 46)

The emergence of Thérèse as the most quoted of the female Saints in the *Catechism* shows that her influence is not on the wane. The publication of this splendid translation of her poems should help renew real devotion to her. In fact, it should play a part in hastening what bishops throughout the world are asking of the Pope, that Thérèse be declared a Doctor of the Church. I hope, too, that it will make people take to heart Thérèse's words when she said she went to Carmel 'above all to pray for priests'.

Throughout these verses truths vital to our faith, particularly in these days, are stressed over and over again. I have been looking at my book on Thérèse, *All Love* (1961). In it I wrote: 'The whole point of Christian charity is that we love men for the sake of God . . . when the world is inverting the order of the two great commandments given us by God a little nun in Normandy sensationally puts things right again . . .':

> This, too, I want (before I go
> To see my Jesus in His Light):
> To win Him countless souls, and so
> To love Him more and more . . .
> > (Poem 10);

to win him souls

> . . . and by the same
> Heart's-fire He came to light them by.
> > (Poem 23)

Thérèse's assertion that because the Church is the Body of Christ it must have a heart and a heart burning with love could well be described as the heart of these poems. Implicit in them, too, is her famous definition which opens the *Catechism's* treatment of prayer (2558) – 'For me, prayer is a surge of the heart; it is a simple look turned toward heaven, it is a cry of recognition and of love, embracing both trial and joy' – and memorable phrases like 'I am not dying, I am entering into life.'

Lovers of Thérèse will find in these poems the singular beauty, unique freshness and beguiling simplicity which throughout her writings illuminate the profundity of her 'Little Way'. Poem after poem sings to me of the Thérèse I have known and loved since I discovered her Act of Offering. She shines more brightly than ever for me now.

Her poems add a wonderful luminosity to all else published, her own writings and writings about her. They make this missionary of spiritual childhood knock at the door of the heart with an apostolic message that is so desperately needed in the sophisticated world of our day. They add to the vital message of our little Saint elements of strength, beauty, truth and love which must result in a richly renewed appreciation. They can only add force to the words of the Bull of Canonization, 'Faithful flock of Christ, the Church offers a new and most noble model of virtue for all of you to contemplate unceasingly.'

CONTENTS

———

Translator's Introduction   XIII

Note to the Reader   XXXIX

Poems   I

Index of Titles   182

Index of First Lines   184

Notes to Translator's Introduction   186

———

TRANSLATOR'S
INTRODUCTION

These are love poems.

When Jean Daujat wrote a book about their author, he called it *Thérèse: la grande amoureuse* – Thérèse: the Great Lover. And Audrey Butler, in a fine phrase used with the poems in mind, has spoken of Thérèse's 'lyric passion for her God'.

But the passionate and the Passion – the blood coughed, the agonized choking, the near-suffocation; whatever (and not necessarily physical) it may turn out to be for oneself – can be complementary, though different, aspects of a love which best expresses itself *by* and through suffering, not in spite of it. The former, the passionate, is much less important than the unrapturous latter (just as a positive response to 'If you love me you will keep my commandments'[1†], is essentially a matter of will, not emotion). Imitation of Christ must not exclude Christ's Crucifixion: which, though it was accepted – sought, indeed – wholly out of love, was not a luxuriantly emotional occasion when the nails tore through the flesh. Acceptance of suffering on one's own part (and with Thérèse it went further than acceptance) can be a love-token, a love-present worth more than words.

St Thérèse

Marie Françoise Thérèse Martin, Sister Thérèse of the Child Jesus, of the Holy Face, died at the age of twenty-four. She, whose last words (in ecstasy, as the bystanders said, before she fell back gently in

---

† The numbers in this Introduction refer to the Notes beginning on page 186.

death) were 'Oh . . . I love him . . . My . . . God! . . . I . . . love . . . you!!', she it was who, in great aridity of spirit, had suffered for months an illness as a result of which, towards the end, her stomach was as hard as a rock and tuberculosis affecting her intestines had led to gangrene.[2]

Those who today know Thérèse well, and as a friend, will need no elaboration from me. For those who do not, I advise the reading, not only of her autobiography, *The Story of a Soul*, and the *Collected Letters*, but also of the *Last Conversations*, a record of her words during the final months of her illness, and *St Thérèse of Lisieux, by those who knew her*, containing testimonies to the diocesan beatification tribunal. (Details of these books are on page 186).

But discard any mental image you have of a soppily sentimental girl. Rather, this was someone tough, in the best sense; intelligent, humorous, deep (simplicity and depth can go together); on any true definition of greatness, a great person, a person *whose response of heart was total*. (Yet we shall hear from her – and it is universally true – that her spiritual achievement, her sanctity, had its continuously flowing well-spring in Another, not herself).

Thérèse's spirituality
It has been truly said that Thérèse loved, not an ideology but a Person:

> White Sacrament I love! Oh come to me,
> Come to me, for my heart aspires to You . . .
>
> Hear, Jesus, as in tenderness I cry:
> 'Come to my heart!'[3]

This love was not initiated by her; one's love of God never is so, for God 'loved us first'.[4] Thérèse recognized (as we all should, but do not) that God loved her, sought her, personally. As well she might be, she was astonished that Christ, true God and true man, not only gives and offers love, but *seeks* it, begs it like a mendicant, in return for His:

> You have, as royal court in Heav'n above,
> The Seraphim – and yet, You beg *my* love . . .[5]

The unreservedness of Thérèse's response was remarkable. She kept nothing back.

'My Love, Divine and little'

'Great is the Lord, and greatly to be praised. Little is the Lord, and greatly to be loved.' Who wrote these words about the Incarnation, I do not know: but Thérèse would have wholly approved of them. For, since her Beloved is both God:

> . . . Grandeur from on high
> Has made me His own abode[6]

and also, astonishingly, One who came down to us as a child in a stable, so Thérèse – like someone turning a jewel this way and that – has to focus, now on one dimension of this unique situation, now on another. God is Father; the Word, co-eternal with the Father and the Holy Spirit, became a child and our brother. Thus, her love for this unique Person, Jesus, is sometimes maternal or sisterly, as when she imagines herself in a boat with the Child and says to him:

> If you want to rest and stay
> As the thunder-rumbles scold –
> Upon me, I beg you! lay
> Your head's little fringe of gold.[7]

Much more often (as we shall see) it is she who is the child, wholly dependent on God: that is the basis of her spirituality.

The littleness of God at Bethlehem, the littleness of God in the

Eucharist, are for Thérèse one: and in the clear light of her simplicity she draws a practical conclusion for her own conduct:

> Hidden as Wafer here, You live for me:
> Jesus, for You I'll also hide away![8]

'. . . it is in the Host that I see You crowning Your self-annihilations . . . For the sake of teaching me humility, You cannot lower Yourself any more . . .'[9]

Jesus, the Bridegroom

> That He and I be one . . .[10]

What is to be said of Thérèse's 'constant betrothal-bridal motif', as V. Sackville-West[11] unsympathetically described it?

> And this I loved: the Host of white
> Came in the morning, to unite
> My soul and His, paid court! And with delight
> I opened – flung its doors apart! –
> My heart.[12]

> . . . My Spouse, my Jesus . . .[13]

> I wear already – look,
> it gleams! – His wedding ring[14]

Though, repeatedly, Thérèse speaks of life on earth as an 'exile', yet:

> Now exile can bring no pain,
> With Him – no wish to be free;
> So soft are the bonds that chain
> Ah, this *Jealous God* and me.[15]

Because Thérèse's vocation was to the life of a Carmelite nun, her use of the nuptial metaphor, which has reference to a union of will and love between the soul and God (of which union on earth there are degrees, degrees of our participation in God's life by sanctifying grace) was set firmly in the setting of the convent: when she speaks of 'spouses of Christ' she means nuns, consecrated in the religious life. But she was familiar with the writings of St John of the Cross, and for him the concept was of wider horizon and referred to a call that is universal. Commenting in the *Spiritual Canticle* on his lines:

> Beneath the apple-tree
> There wert thou betrothed,

he says that the apple-tree[16] 'is the wood of the Cross, where the Son of God . . . betrothed our human nature to Himself, *and, by consequence, every soul of man.*'[17] (St Bernard realistically adds that some souls 'are not in need of a Bridegroom but of a heavenly doctor';[18] and, as for those who attain to their destiny, Thérèse herself reminds us that a thimble-glass and a large tumbler can both be full to the brim with 'as much glory as they can take').[19]

The nuptial metaphor *is* only a metaphor, of course, though an apt one. For it has not 'entered into the heart of man, what things God hath prepared for them that love him.'[20] Of the perfection of union with God, in heaven – our high and eternal destiny as individuals if we achieve it – St John the Evangelist can only say that 'we shall be like' Him.[21] 'The immense riches that God possesses by nature,' wrote Ruysbroeck, 'we may possess by virtue of love . . .'.[22] The Mystical Body of Christ, his Bride, is made up of countless individual members.

Though St Thérèse is a Saint of the ordinary in a way that St John of the Cross is not, we can apply to her Maritain's words about the latter. To her readers, *us*, she reveals, 'depicted with strokes of flame, the real way to tear off and cast aside the . . . pretence of our wretched masquerade, telling them in one word for what they have been created.'[23]

On the morning of his execution, St John Fisher said it was his 'wedding day'.

Annihilation of one's own will – Transformation

It is not a marriage of equals, this entry into the 'family' of God, here and in heaven. The disproportion is dizzying, yet not such as should daunt us. To her hesitating cousin, Marie Guérin, Thérèse wrote: 'You seem to me like a little village girl whom a mighty king comes to ask in marriage and who does not dare accept on the pretext that she is not rich enough, or trained enough in the usages of court; without reflecting that her royal fiancé knows her poverty and her weakness much better than she knows it herself . . .'[24]

There is no ambiguity about Thérèse's descriptions of her Lover and loved one: He is true God and true man. When still a baby, in the arms of Mary on the flight to Egypt or at Nazareth, He every moment:

> . . . upheld the world
> by keeping it in mind[25].

And, for Thérèse (wholly scriptural, wholly Catholic, in her theology) Christ's sufferings and death made available to us the very life of the Trinity, the 'family life' of God. For one who would love Jesus:

> Father and Son his Visitants shall be . . .[26]

By baptism (Thérèse makes St Cecilia say to Valerian):

> The True and Only God will live in you indeed!
> The Holy Spirit . . . He will animate you then.[27]

The uniqueness of the other Person in the marriage-betrothal brought an apt response from Thérèse. In recognition of that uniqueness and her creatureship and dependency, she relies utterly on the loving God, the omnipotent. She retains her personality, as she must (and how delightful a one it is!) but gives up entirely what Marmion calls 'the proprietorship' of her activity, her life. In that sense, she wants to be lost in God, as a drop of water loses itself in a great sea. She seeks a total annihilation of her own will: 'Yes, I want Him to take over my faculties in such a way that I no longer perform any human and personal actions, but actions wholly divine and directed by the Spirit of Love.'[28] In this only is to be found her fulfilment, here as well as in eternity:

> Love's fire! consume me ruthlessly . . .[29]

> Fresh altar-roses, Lord,
> > are gratified to shine –
> Self-gifts we *see*! –
> Instead of that *I* would
> > (this other dream is mine)
> Un-petal me . . .[30]

Of the Heart of Jesus:

> You know – all my desires to You are known –
> I want my being to be lost in It![31]

> Fire burns inside my soul; it came
> My heart – for always! – to endue.
> I walk in Love's enchanting flame.
> It always will consume me through.[32]

Comparing us to altar-breads before the Consecration in the Mass, she says that Jesus:

> ... desires
> To change *us* into Him as well.[33]

> Flame-drawn, the wingèd insect (see!)
> Will hurtle to the fire ... [34]

'In order to live in one act of perfect Love, *I offer myself as a victim of holocaust to Your* MERCIFUL LOVE, beseeching You to consume me ceaselessly, letting overflow into my soul the waves of *infinite tenderness* which are contained in You, that thus I may become a *Martyr* of your *Love*, O my God! . . . I want, O my Beloved, with each beat of my heart to renew to You this offering an infinite number of times . . .'[35]

Centre of reliance

As Blosius pointed out, indignation at one's own imperfections is often the effect of self-love;[36] we are disturbed when the bogus perfection of our pharisaical self-image is shown (by ourselves to ourselves, even) to be less than complete.

Thérèse's self-image is humbler and finer. 'I see my weakness, but it gives me no distress,' she writes in a poem addressed to Mary, the human Mother given to us by God.[37] Thérèse does not belittle sin (that is, offences against God). Much less does she belittle serious sin; rejection of God's love fills her with horror and she has a 'thirst' to 'save sinners' through her suffering. At the same time she distinguishes our sins from our sillinesses and our indeliberate 'faults which do not OFFEND Him' but merely have 'the effect of humbling oneself and making love stronger.'[38] 'I will have the right, without offending the good God, to do little stupid things up to my death, if I am humble, if I stay very little. Look at little children: they never stop breaking things, tearing things, falling down, all whilst loving their parents very, very much.'[39]

Some spiritual persons examine the 'escutcheons' of their past lives and even though the blots have been wholly wiped away by

God's forgiveness and absolution (which, rightly, they do not doubt), they nevertheless *torment* themselves at the fact that blots were ever there; almost as though on the self-regarded 'escutcheon' the blots were there still. Thérèse will have none of this:

> Living by Love means banishing all fear –
> All glancing-back to faults of earlier day:
> Of my past sins I see no imprint here,
> Love in a trice has burnt them all away![40]

She speaks of the tender God:

> . . . loving me – my frailty no less,
> The whole of me![41]

> I know this as reality:
> The good, the bad in me – the whole,
> Love's Power draws profit from, for He
> Into *Himself* transforms my soul.[42]

Paradoxically, a recognition of one's own nothingness and a surrender to the Mercy of God bring liberation, since reliance on God (who can be relied on) replaces the desire for a self-justification that is non-existent, illusory.

During her last illness Thérèse 'saw through the window the setting sun casting its last fires over nature, and the top of the trees appeared all golden. I said to myself then: What a difference if one stays in the shade or, on the contrary, opens oneself to the sun of Love . . . Then, one appears all golden. In reality I am not that, and I would cease to be that immediately if I withdrew myself from Love.'[43] It was impossible, said Thérèse – not difficult, 'impossible'[44] – to do anything of supernatural worth by herself:

> I know, in all our acts of justice, we
> Have nothing that's of value to You, so
> My sacrifices . . . all! as in a sea –
> To give them worth – into Your Heart I throw . . .[45]

It was utterly necessary for her (as it is for us) to have an 'ascenseur' – an elevator, a lift; a parent who comes specially down from the top of the stairs and carries the infant up.[46] It is St Paul's 'Gladly therefore will I glory in my infirmities, that the power of Christ may dwell in me.'[47] And it is John Henry Newman's:

> Simply to His grace and wholly
> Light and life and strength belong,
> And I love, supremely, solely,
> Him the holy, Him the strong.[48]

'The saints have always had a lively awareness that their merits were pure grace': *Catechism of the Catholic Church*, 2011, quoting Thérèse's Act of Offering.

Her 'little way' is the way of humility; of a child who, knowing its littleness, does not pretend to be big. Humility simply recognizes reality – the reality of who and what God is and who and what we are. Human pride ridiculously struts in unreality, in untruth.[49] 'Littleness', Thérèse insists, is the only way to make spiritual progress; one must descend to ascend[50]: He must increase, I decrease.[51] 'As soon as He sees us really convinced of our own nothingness . . . He stretches out His hand to us; but if we want to try to do some great thing, even under the pretext of zeal, He leaves us alone.'[52]

> 'I . . . am the one who stunts tall trees and
> makes the low ones grow' (Ezekiel 17:24)[53]

Like Elizabeth of the Trinity after her, Thérèse said that 'our mission is to forget ourselves . . .';[54] her heart, she wrote, had to be 'wholly empty of me.'[55] (But one loved by God is not a 'no-one', and that is the true basis of self-esteem.)

Thérèse's loving was entirely by grace and entirely by free will (for grace perfects nature and does not destroy the freedom of our wills). But even the love she gives to God, Thérèse regards as having come in the first place from God, who asks for the love of our free wills in return. I will love You, she says to Jesus:

> with such Love – the very same –
> As I received, O Son of God, from You.[56]

The thirteenth-century mystic, Blessed Angela of Foligno, wrote: 'And I understood that He desired the soul to love Him, with that same love with which He loved the soul, according to her power and strength' – her capacity – 'and that, *according to her desire*, so would He fill her up' as a vessel is filled. '. . . I saw I had nothing good belonging to me. And in that way I saw that it was not I who loved, however much I might see myself to be in love, but that the love was God's alone, with which He reunited Himself, and then conferred more and more ardent love than before; and I had a great desire to become one with this love.'[57]

Confidence in Divine Mercy – Spiritual Childhood – Surrender

'Trust' – confidence – and 'total surrender'[58] were the words Thérèse used to summarize her 'way of spiritual childhood'. ('Surrender' does not quite translate the French *abandon*, which suggests a glorious lack of inhibition, of holding back, as in 'doing something with abandon'.) We can see why she used these words; they describe the relationship of a child – a helpless, *little* child – to its loving parents. 'To stay little is . . . to expect everything from the good God, as a very little child expects everything from its Father. It is not worrying about anything . . .'[59]

She holds out 'empty hands'[60] as a child in its simplicity does. 'I know well that I shall never be worthy of what I am hoping for; but I stretch out my hand to You like a little beggar' – a child with its hand out – 'and I am sure you will grant my wishes fully, for You are so good.'[61] For her, prayer is 'an upsurge of heart, a simple look thrown towards Heaven,'[62] habitually; and Jesus, she said, gives her what she needs spiritually, as she needs it, without her knowing how.[63]

God as a father, God as a lover . . . all the emphasis is upon tenderness and Divine Mercy. His Love in fact is All-mercy; stooping lovingly to our weakness, gratuitous. God is Justice also (hence her concern at and for sinners who reject Him). But justice and mercy are not separated: 'What a sweet joy to think that the good God is *Just*; that's to say, that He takes our weaknesses into account, that He knows perfectly the frailty of our nature.'[64]

Using words which on first publication after her death were attributed (dubiously) to St Augustine, Thérèse calls surrender 'the delicious fruit of love':

> It gives me, here below,
> Repose – a sea of peace . . . [65]

> My Saviour, I'm caressed,
> I'm lulled, upon the breast
>   Of You, my All.[66]

She is a child, loved, 'dandled'[67] upon the knee; a lover, loved:

> One sees it – on the wings of prayer
> The ardent heart is soaring high,
> As when the lark – in upper air –
> Sings as it rises in the sky.[68]

> Here, in your home, I stay and will not move;
> Singing, by your hearth-blaze in restfulness:
>   'I live by Love!'[69]

Active response

But it would be wholly, ludicrously, wrong to think of her as lapsing into quietism;[70] a child sitting back on the shore and letting the waves of love lap over her. Ten thousand times, no! As Victor Sion[71] says, 'She never uses her weakness as an excuse to avoid an effort.' (A violinist, who at first may practise laboriously, still requires to make a *great* effort – for correctness of fingering and precision of bowing – even when he is relaxedly surrendering himself to the music.)

One of Thérèse's poems, 'The Story of a Shepherdess become Queen' (ostensibly about the novice, Sr Marie-Madeleine, but every poem says something about Thérèse herself) speaks of the shepherdess hearing the call to Carmel, and:

> Hearing, the shepherdess at once
> In joy, sets out and will not stop;
> Led by her Mother, Mary – runs . . .[72]

'*Runs*' . . . Though it is translator's poetic licence which admits that precise word, not explicitly in the French, there could be no better word[73] to characterize Thérèse's response in love; and not only as regards her entry to 'the little Carmel of Lisieux'. What marked the whole of her life there was her alacrity and (in the words of her sister, Pauline) 'a most generous attentiveness to seize every opportunity of doing acts pleasing to God.'[74]

Poverty, obedience, virginity, all involved renunciation; but the renunciation was eager, not grudging, there was no 'I wish I did not have to':

> But no created being could I find
> Who here on earth would love me deathlessly . . .[75]

What is to be seen in her, daily, is not passivity, not formality only, but what Monseigneur Guy Gaucher[76] has called 'the dynamism of love'. In her day, no doubt, the Lisieux Carmel's general observance

of the letter and spirit of the Rule under Mère Marie de Gonzague –
a Prioress so severe in some things – was not all it should have been.
But she, Thérèse, has her own promptings of heart; she is there to
love; and, for her, love means giving without reserve:

> . . . I have stopped all counting up. I see
> That when one loves, one doesn't measure out![77]

> You want my heart – it's here! I utterly
> Cede my desires to You . . .[78]

And (one says again) not only in passive acceptance:

> Come sword or fire, next *Him* I'll stay serene –
> I'll rush to the arena fearlessly . . . [79]

Of the Blessed Virgin:

> . . . I would strive, but sing as she![80]

Nor is this simply rhetoric. In little things and great, Thérèse showed
her love actively and in practical ways. Every little external act, done
as well as she could, every hidden sacrifice, great or little, was – not
self-directed perfectionism, but – a love-present from her to God.
For her, obedience to the Rule, obedience to her religious Superior
(even an odd and capricious Superior like Mère Gonzague) was
obedience to God, whom the Superior represented. This is why, for
example, when engaged in writing she ends in mid-phrase[81] on the
bell ringing. And whilst words were important to her (one who is in
love cannot stop talking about the beloved), words alone would not
do: she had to *prove* her love for Christ in everything, including
loving her fellow-nuns with Christ's love, even (indeed, especially)
those few individuals who, on the natural level, set her teeth on edge
by their mannerisms.[82]

She did not think up artificial penances for herself; as with us, there were plenty to hand in her daily living. In her hidden spiritual life she wanted to make use of every opportunity that came her way. At the age of fourteen, she wrote, she had wished 'to *love* Jesus *passionately*, to give Him a thousand tokens of love whilst I still could.'[83] This wish never left her. Sister Thérèse, said one of her novices, 'transformed all her actions, even the most insignificant, into acts of love.'[84]

She does not count up her good deeds. 'Give away your [spiritual] goods in the measure you get them.'[85] What she is concerned to do is 'to abandon herself, to give herself up, without keeping anything, not even the joy of knowing how much the bank is paying out.'[86]

She loved the Church: she wished, by uncompromising obedience to Christ's Mystical Body on earth, to love and obey Christ. One of her novices expressed such a firm belief in her Little Way that if the Pope himself 'were to tell me you had been mistaken, I couldn't believe him.' Thérèse replied bluntly, 'Oh! You should believe the Pope above all . . .'[87] (One could do with more of that among Catholics today.)

'To slake the burning . . .'
Though the love which she expresses by the actions of her daily life is for Christ personally, the relationship is not restricted to 'I – You': her love of Him radiates towards others, *for* Him. She offers her daily sacrifices for priests, for missionaries; she is apostolic and strives to gain grace for others:

> That Blaze from Heav'n! – into my soul it came;
> I want to spread its burnings all about . . .[88]

> I came to Carmel – why?
> *To people Heaven* . . .[89]

> The more I feel Your Flame,
>   the more I've got to do

> To slake the burning. How?
>> In giving souls to You![90]

> This harvest-gift of love –
>> with souls for grapes . . . [91]

Again looking back on her feelings at fourteen, Thérèse wrote: 'I wanted to give my Beloved to drink and I felt myself consumed with a *thirst* for *souls* . . .'[92] 'It was a true exchange of love . . . the more I gave Him to *drink,* the more the thirst of my poor little soul increased and it was this ardent thirst He gave me as the most delightful draught of His love.'[93]

'Delightful draught'! Lest anyone should think that her life in Carmel was packed with perpetual ecstasies, one has here to stress that rather was it one of daily aridity and worse: for a period, the desolate absence of any *feeling* about the very existence of life beyond the grave, utter darkness. There was 'a wall reaching right up to Heaven, shutting out the stars.'[94] But:

> . . . adoring You
>> in dark but loving state;
> I'll see You when it's dawn,
>> O Jesus! – I will wait.[95]

In her darkness and trial[96] she had lost feeling, not faith. Lacking consolation, she sang 'simply what *I want to believe*' when she sang in her poems 'of the happiness of Heaven, the eternal possession of God.'[97] She was in a 'black hole,' soul and body,[98] (and one should not minimize the desolation and horror of it), but nevertheless, way down, 'in an astonishing peace'.[99]

Suffering

When Thérèse wrote that her 'joy' was in suffering for Christ, she did not mean (in her own phrase) '*felt* joy.'[100] She meant 'peace'; and

'To suffer in peace it is enough to will, very much, everything that Jesus wills.'[101] Writing to her sister, Céline, she said: 'He would rather see you stub yourself against the stones of the path by night than walk in broad daylight along a road made colourful with flowers which could slow your advance.'[102]

Describing her First Communion, Thérèse remarked that at that stage Jesus made no demands of her; there had been 'no struggles, no sacrifices',[103] no physical suffering. Later it was otherwise; Monseigneur Gaucher, in his book *The Passion of Thérèse of Lisieux*,[104] has given us a moving description. On the one hand she never sought suffering, of herself and apart from God: 'I am very glad I have never asked the good God for anything;[105] that way, He is forced to give me courage.'[106] 'If I were to ask for sufferings, these would be my sufferings, *mine*; I would have to bear them alone, and I've never been able to do anything alone.'[107]

And yet, since the more suffering came her way, the more she could prove her love (and the more fruitful her apostolate of grace would be) – in that sense, and for those reasons, she desired more suffering; she uses the word *réclamer*, ask for, claim, even beg for:

> I ask for suffering: the Cross
> I love – desire! Ah, well you know –
> To save one soul from final loss
> A thousand deaths I'd undergo![108]

Thérèse's attitude to suffering is well summarized in the quotation from Père Jamart given in the notes to Poem 30, on page 117. Her motives, varied but related, all spring from love:

> It's in the Winepress – Suffering –
> That I'll be proving what I say . . .'[109]

> . . . *That suffering has charms* my heart knows too;
> One can save sinners – through the Cross, this is![110]

[XXIX]

Suffering was not sought – much less is it permitted by God – for its own sake. Among its mysterious attributes is the fact that through our sufferings (which pass) we can participate voluntarily in Christ's saving work. In her daily life as a Carmelite, Thérèse offered herself especially for this. 'Jesus,' she wrote, 'made me understand that it was through the cross that He wished to give me souls' – and she to give souls to Him – 'and my attraction for suffering grew in proportion as the suffering increased.'[111] Loving Him, she loved others in seeking, above all, to make them love Him too.

She desired suffering as a way of returning love to One who on earth had suffered for her:

> To be like You is my desire,
> So what I ask is suffering . . .'[112]

> To suffer, silently, so I'll
> Give Jesus comfort – that's my will.[113]

To 'give Jesus comfort': as though, in His agony in Gethsemane, she would stretch out her hand to Him and say, 'I am here.'

Thérèse was 'Sister Thérèse, of the Child Jesus, *of the Holy Face*'. That last description evoked for her a picture of the Man of Sorrows, and she sought especially to suffer like Him in order to accomplish His will to save souls.[114] Read Manuscript B in the autobiography for a glowing exposition of Thérèse's vocation: love. Read the *Last Conversations* to see how she has come to a state in which she wants – not just accepts, positively wants – only what her Loved One wants. The scales of her own wishes are in equilibrium between dying soon or living longer . . . whichever He wills.[115]

Fulfilment

The only true fulfilment of a human being is eternal possession of God whose heart-filling loveliness does not, cannot, satiate.

'The loving soul, for the sake of greater conformity with the

Beloved, cannot cease to desire the recompense and reward of its love for the sake of which it serves the Beloved, otherwise it could not be true love . . .' (St John of the Cross, *Spiritual Canticle*).[116]

From her sick-bed, during her excruciating last illness, Thérèse could occasionally hear music coming from somewhere in Lisieux. 'This evening,' she said to her sister, Pauline, 'I heard some music in the distance, and I was thinking that I would soon be hearing incomparable melodies . . .'[117]

'Soon Faith will take and tear apart her veil . . .'[118]

'Arise, make haste, my love, my dove, my beautiful one, and come. For winter is now past, the rain is over and gone. The flowers have appeared in our land . . .'[119]

Thérèse wanted, she said, 'to die of love,' but 'To die of love is not to die in transports.'[120] Among her last words were, 'All I have written about my desire for suffering is quite true; I do not regret my being delivered up to Love . . .'[121] 'Oh! I wouldn't want to suffer for a shorter time!'[122] And then, at her last moment (like the sun-burst of sound in Elgar's *Gerontius* when the human soul glimpses God face to face): 'Oh! . . . I love him . . . My . . . God! . . . I . . . love you!'[123]

> You'll see Him gaze at you – the night
> Will be ablaze that once was black!
> You'll fly to Heav'n, in high delight,
> With nothing now to hold you back![124]

A remarkable statement: 'Until the end of the world . . .'

And yet her 'rest' in Heaven, is an active one! On the morning of 17 July 1897 – she had just coughed up blood – Thérèse had said: 'I feel I'm about to enter into rest. But I feel above all that my mission is about to begin, my mission of making God loved as I love Him, of giving my little way to souls. If God grants my desires, my Heaven will be spent on earth until the end of the world. Yes, I want to spend my Heaven doing good on earth. This isn't impossible, since from the very bosom of the beatific vision the angels watch over us. I can't throw myself into a spree of enjoyment, I don't want to rest as long as there are souls to be saved . . . But when the Angel will have said, "Time is no more!", then I shall rest, I shall be able to enjoy myself, because the number of the elect will be complete and all will have entered into joy and into rest. My heart thrills at this thought.'[125]

Hans Urs von Balthasar comments on this extraordinary statement as follows: 'Thérèse rediscovers the ancient patristic conception of heaven, one to some extent shared by the Middle Ages and according to which the saints in heaven are in a transitory state until the Last Judgment. Not until all the members of the Mystical Body are gathered together can the whole Body of Christ rise again; not until the last of the awaited brethren enters into the Kingdom can the heavenly throng cease to bend over the earth with care.' (But 'even this transitory state before the Last Judgement is really and truly heaven', and Thérèse does not doubt that, any more than the early Christian Fathers did.)[126]

Thérèse is, as it were, an active, dynamic saint; demonstrative, often, to those who ask her for things. The huge number of spiritual and physical cures and other remarkable answers attributable to her intercession seems certainly to be a Divine confirmation of a mission to articulate and then to spread her 'little way', rooted as it is in the Gospel.

The poems and the translations

Thérèse's poems were written between February 1893 and July 1897, the year of her death. Her fellow-nuns in the Lisieux convent knew she wrote poems; she wrote some of them for individual members of the community who had asked her to express their own ideas in verse. (Even those poems are rich in Thérèse's spirituality: the developed thoughts are hers.) Yet her fellow-nuns – other than her sisters, Pauline, Marie and Céline, and Mère Marie de Gonzague – had no idea,[127] until after her death, that Thérèse had written her autobiography (on which she set to work from religious obedience).

Among English-speaking readers today, the position is reversed, almost. There are good English translations of the autobiography, but for those who do not read French the poems are virtually unknown, except through prose translations of short extracts or verse translations of the more celebrated of the poems. In the early part of this century, two English verse translations of the greater number of those poems which had appeared in French editions of the autobiography (from 1898 onwards) emanated from translators in the United States. Both these verse translations are now out of print, and in literary terms neither was an outstanding success.

Not that Thérèse's poems in the original French are regarded as great *literary* works by French critics: in the latter's view this line is *'faible'*, that phrase 'maladroit'. My English ear can neither confirm nor deny the validity of such judgments, but if they are correct, then I simply say 'So be it.' For me, as for those same French critics, it is in their content that the real interest of the poems lies. I think they are great love-poems, and so distinctive as to be incomparable.[128]

All but one of the fifty poems here translated were first published in 1898, in an appendix to Thérèse's autobiography, *Histoire d'une Ame*. Mère Agnès, Thérèse's sister Pauline, prepared that volume for publication; and, making use of an authority Thérèse had given her[129] – and with encouragement and aid from two priests of the Abbey of Mondaye – she altered words and phrases in a desire to improve the poems. She did improve the French composition of some passages, and frequently the poetry. In some places, by her alterations, she brought out, enhanced, the very meaning (or the overtones of the meaning) intended by Thérèse. For example, in Poem 26, stanza 5, she added the words *ici-bas* (here below). The change is minor, but it gives a new resonance – the Incarnation, and Christ's parentage : His mother, on earth; His Father, in heaven – of which Thérèse would surely have approved. This example could be multiplied.

In some passages what at first might be taken to be phrases wholly Pauline's own are in fact phrases used elsewhere by Thérèse herself.[130] But sometimes Pauline was simply not in touch with Thérèse's mind. Sometimes she was timid where Thérèse was bold; and some-times she brought the soaring bird down to earth. For example, in the poem here numbered 8 (stanza 10) she changed 'gentle' (*douces*) chains to 'noble' chains, thus replacing with opaqueness and conventiality what in Thérèse's manuscript had been delicate and original. However, these changes are comparatively minor (especially in their effect on an English verse translation). Pauline did not over-edit the poems to the degree she did the autobiography.

In 1979, *Un Cantique d'amour* (Paris: Les Editions du Cerf et Desclée de Brouwer), an édition intégrale of Thérèse's poems in two volumes, produced by a distinguished group of scholars, was published. In forty of the poems Thérèse's manuscript words and phrases have been restored to the text, and in addition (also from the manuscripts) there are twenty-two of her poems which did not appear in *Histoire d'une Ame*, and voluminous critical notes. *Un Cantique d'amour* must be regarded as containing the definitive French text, and so valuable are the critical notes that it is good to know that an English translation is being brought out by ICS Publications, Washington, D.C. The present little volume does not attempt to rival that great critical work; its aim is devotional.

Un Cantique d'amour did not include the poems which Thérèse wrote for the 'pious recreations', the name given to the plays (some in prose, some in verse, some a mixture of the two) which she composed for the nuns to act in the Lisieux Carmel on feast-days. Certain of those poems appeared in the appendix to *Histoire d'une Ame*. A critical edition of all the plays was published in 1985 under the title *Théâtre au Carmel* (Paris: Cerf DDB).

The present book includes nine of these 'poems from the plays'. References to 'PN' (*poésie numéro*) and 'PS' (*poésie supplémentaire*) are references to the numbering in *Un Cantique d'amour*. References to 'RP' (*récréations pieuses*) are references to the numbering in *Théâtre au Carmel*. The date given after each poem is the date or approximate date stated in those works.

Altogether I have translated seventy-one of Thérèse's poems; this book contains fifty of them. Notwithstanding restrictive copyright and translation rights vested elsewhere than in Lisieux, I hope that I may publish the remainder of my translations at some time in the future. As regards the fifty poems in this book, I have translated generally from the 1898 text as edited by Pauline. Many of the differences between the two texts, 1898 and 1979 (1985), do not affect the English translation at all, and, of those that do, some – unindicated – are in my view quite immaterial as regards both meaning and poetry. In a relatively small number of cases – around 55 words altogether (the largest number of these in Poem 17) out of a total number of words between 18,000 and 19,000 – I have incorporated 'restored manuscript' words or phrases where to have omitted them would have resulted in a distortion of Thérèse's meaning. In the case of other differences which seem to me to matter, but not as much, I have adopted the following device. A star in the margin indicates those notes which draw attention to what I regard as (more or less) significant deviations by Pauline from Thérèse's original manuscript intentions.

The majority of the starred notes give merely a general indication of what Thérèse's manuscript wording was, for which Pauline – or possibly a priest associate – substituted what was thought to be improved wording. This, I think, is sufficient for a book with the objectives of this one. To see *precisely* what the manuscript words were in those cases – as well as for valuable notes on the poems – the reader is recommended to refer to *Un Cantique d'amour* (Vol. I, and especially Vol. II which gives the precise differences between the two versions) and to *Théâtre au Carmel*. To the French and U.S. publishers named above I am happy to give acknowledgement of the limited use of restored material from the manuscripts, an acknowledgement which extends to some short quotations, in my own translation, from French material still in copyright which I use in the commentary to illuminate Thérèse's thought and/or to point to parallels between the poems and other works of Thérèse. I make acknowledgement also to the Office Central de Lisieux in respect of short passages translated by me from the manuscript autobiography published by them. I acknowledge in their individual places the sources of short quotations from other copyright material.

The starred notes, then, are not a substitute for a perusal of the 1979 and 1985 texts (and the critical notes which accompany them) in *Un Cantique d'amour* and *Théâtre au Carmel*. The present book is not a critical edition. It aims at conveying something of the 'music' of Thérèse's hymns of love.

Principles of this translation

Thérèse's poems are natural and unsophisticated – often almost conversational – even where her chosen phraseology is stylized and 'poetic'. I have tried to reproduce this in the translations, whilst retaining, I hope, a *fin de siècle* feel. The translation is not always literal, but my aim has been to reproduce Thérèse's thoughts with exactitude. My judgment may be at fault, but if I have omitted any word or phrase it is because I thought it inessential to her meaning; if I have included in the English something not explicitly in the French, it is because I thought that my words followed naturally from the actual French words.

The rhyme-*scheme* of each translation is exactly that of the French original. I have followed Thérèse's metres too, to this extent at least: that each line has the same number of syllables as in the French. Of course these English verses, with their traditional regularity of stress, are aimed at the English ear. Except in the case of the alexandrines, I have not sought systematically to reproduce the caesurae or internal breaks of rhythm found in the French. I add that where lines of (say) eight syllables in the French could conceivably be translated as trippingly anapaestic three-stress lines or as more stately four-stress lines, I have preferred the latter.

These are the poems of a young woman. As I have done in the translations, Thérèse used exclamation marks frequently (though mine in the English are not necessarily in the same places as hers in the French); and when she underlines, italicizes, she does it in order to emphasize the importance of something already made clear, whereas generally[131] I have italicized in order to bring out the meaning itself. However, the parenthetic style of the translations, and the practice of having an unimportant word at the end of a line (as a kind of springboard for the line which follows), are mine and not hers.

It may not be out of place to say how I came to embark on the translations. When attending Monsignor Francis Horsfield's pilgrimage-retreat in Lisieux in 1992, I was seized – I cannot describe it otherwise – with a desire, an impulsion, to translate the poems (which at that stage I had not even read). On the way home to England – as, with my wife, I climbed the steep hill to the Chapel of Notre Dame de Grâce at Honfleur (where, in July 1887, Thérèse, accompanied by her father and her sisters Léonie and Céline, prayed that she might be allowed to enter Carmel at an early age) – I was already 'tasting' in my mind English phrases that might translate a particular French stanza, picked at random, from Poem 17, *Vivre d'Amour*.

Then quatrain by quatrain, in the early morning, translations emerged over the next twelve months. If I say that I think Thérèse helped me, I hope I shall not be thought fanciful (in fact, I sometimes feel that 'helped' is an understatement). Indeed, considering my lack of fluency in French when I began the translations, I think I could not have completed the task otherwise.

Acknowledgements

I wish to express my most grateful thanks to successive Mother Prioresses of the Lisieux Carmel and the respective Sisters in charge of the Theresian Archives; the Office Central de Lisieux; Father John A. Feeley (formerly of The Catholic University of America, Washington, D.C.), whose presence in Lisieux was truly providential and whose assessment of the translations, and advice, were so valuable; and, in England, to Canon Francis J. Ripley and the Community of the St Helens Carmel, for their help, encouragement and prayers.

I am deeply in debt to Audrey Butler who, with her husband Arnold, read the translations in typescript at an early stage, and who both lifted my spirits through her reaction to them and helped me by her constructive suggestions. Judith Swarbrick, as librarian, and the Preston Carmel by the loan of books, assisted me much. I am grateful also to Carole Allsopp for her expert and patient secretarial work; to Paul Burns for much sagacious guidance; to Giles Semper and Murray White, successive editors at HarperCollins*Religious* along with Rosamund Webber and (as regards design and typography) Linde Hardaker and Vicky Marquina; and, for important help in specific areas, Véronique Strassel, Laurence Quesney and Barbara Dziurowicz.

Finally, I would like to record my delight at one fact. Dr Thomas Holland, retired bishop of the Salford diocese, where I live (I had the pleasure of talking with him whilst this work was in preparation) met Thérèse's sisters Pauline and Céline, not in the pages of a book but in actuality; in 1944, at the liberation of France, when he was a naval chaplain and they had just returned to the Lisieux Carmel from their temporary refuge in the crypt of the Basilica.

I feel, somehow, that over the months of translating I have had the honour of meeting Thérèse almost no less personally.

**Feast of SS John Fisher and
Thomas More, 1995**

NOTE TO THE READER

———

Pronunciation

Words like 'flower' which could be one syllable or two are pronounced as the metre dictates. Thus in Poem 1, stanza 3 (line 1) 'Flower' is monosyllabic: but by the time one reaches stanza 4 (line 5) that word has opened out into two syllables, like the very bloom it describes.

A word like 'flower' at the end of a line (as in stanza 2) is to be pronounced as a monosyllable.

As with words which could be one syllable or two, so with words which could be two syllables or three, etc. The metre dictates, for example, that 'radiance' (which in other places might be two syllables) shall in stanza 1 be an expansive three syllables, and that 'Sanctuary' in stanza 5 shall be four.

Some words, e.g. 'Heaven' (a word which appears many times in Thérèse's poems) are printed either 'Heaven' or 'Heav'n', to make their pronunciation clear at a glance.

Layout of lines

As in the French, some of the lines are *alexandrines*, consisting of twelve syllables (six English feet). There is a break of rhythm, near-imperceptible or longer, at the end of the sixth syllable (third foot).

These regular breaks of rhythm are signalled in two ways. Where an entire poem or an entire stanza is made up of alexandrines, the break is indicated by the symbol ', as in Poem 2. Otherwise, it is indicated by the splitting of the line, three feet upper, three feet lower, as in Poem 5.

Key

To the Notes at the foot of each poem, the following key applies:

Aut.   Thérèse's autobiography
1.   line
Ms.   Manuscript
P   Pauline (Mère Agnès)
St.   stanza
Th   Thérèse

POEMS

[I]

THE DIVINE DEW or
THE VIRGINAL MILK OF MARY

1   My gentle Jesus, on Your Mother's breast
I see You, as a *radiance* of Love!
That mystery, whose depth can not be guessed,
Made You an exile from Your Home above.
Ah, let me hide where, in that veil, You are
Removed from mortal gaze; let it be giv'n
To me, that close to You, O Morning Star,
I find in it a foretaste, here, of Heav'n!

2   Since first – at break of dawn's awaking-hour –
A sudden flare of sun the darkness rends,
The tender bud that's turning to a flower
Is waiting till a precious balm descends.
It's *dew*, the kindly dew! – when morning breaks,
What freshness does this moisture bring about!
Producing sap abundantly, it makes
The budded petals start to open out.

3   You, Jesus, are the Flower just open new –
I think of Your first waking and see this.
You, Jesus! – that delightful Rose is You:
In that vermilion bud, what grace there is!
Your sinless Mother, rocking You to rest,
Makes of her arms a royal throne for You.
What is Your gentle sun but Mary's breast?
What other than the Virgin's milk, Your dew?

4 My Love, Divine and little! I can see
  The future in Your face, dear Brother: how
  You'll leave – and soon – Your Mother's side, for me;
  Love presses You to suffer, even now.
  But on the Cross, full-opened Flower! You
  Afford me of Your morning Scent a sign:
  I recognize what this is – Mary's dew,
  The Virgin's milk, this is . . . Your Blood divine!

5 Here, in the holy Sanctuary! where ★¹
  The angels wonder, and their joy is told;
  In offering to God their soaring prayer,
  They keep repeating, like St John: 'Behold!'.
  The Word-made-Host – ah, yes! behold Him who
  Is Lamb and Priest eternally. We're fed
  The Son of God, who's Son of Mary too:
  The Virgin's Milk, this is . . . the Angels' Bread!

6 It's glory that the Seraphs feed upon –
  Pure happiness of love, in Paradise. ★²
  But I'm a child, and weak; Communion
  Brings just the image *milk* before my eyes.
  That's right for childhood, though! – and to out-tower
  All else, the Love of Jesus a delight.
  O tender Love! Unfathomable Power!
  The Virgin's milk, this is . . . my Host of white!

Notes

PN 1

2 February 1893, Feast of the Purification

'. . . the forget-me-not need only half-open, or rather lift up its wreath of petals, in order that the *Bread* of *Angels* may come like a Divine Dew to strengthen it and give it all it lacks' (Thérèse, letter to Sr Marie of the Trinity, June 1897).

Thérèse's first poem. She has been in Carmel since April 1888. Mère Marie de Gonzague is Prioress, but is about to be succeeded in that office by Thérèse's sister, Pauline (Sr Agnès de Jésus). Another Thérèse in the community, Sr Thérèse de Saint-Augustin, has a strong personal devotion to the Holy Infancy, the babyhood of Christ. She asks Thérèse to write a poem on the subject. According to her account, Thérèse at first hesitates: 'I know nothing about poetry . . . I don't know if it's the will of God.'

★[1] By deleting some words of Th, P omitted the former's reference to the Eucharist as the *hidden* Christ.

★[2] P (quite appositely) added the words 'pure love' to Th's reference to the Seraphs' perfect happiness.

JOAN AT DOMRÉMY
(from a play about Joan of Arc)

After hearing, in the fields, her voices –
St Catherine, St Margaret and St Michael
– Joan delivers her response:

For love of You, my God! ' for that alone I go –
Depart my father's house, ' and parents very dear –
For You, I go to war! ' I leave my vale, and, oh,
The lovely village-bell, ' the flock I guarded here.
I'll lead the *army* now, ' and not these lambs of mine,
No longer shall I play ' with pretty flowers, Lord!
My joy, my eighteen Springs, ' I give You. As a sign –
To please You, God, this hand ' will reach out for a sword!
My singing-voice, that joined ' the breeze that rose and fell,
10   Must, like a steeple-clang, ' above the shouting rise:
No more the dreamy sound of ' that uncertain bell –
For, louder, I shall hear ' a people's battle-cries.
Yes! Sacrifice I love. ' The cross is my desire:
Ah, call me now for this – ' to suffer! Here am I.
To suffer, loving You! ' With joy I am on fire.
O Jesus – Master! Love! ' for You I want to die.   ★

Notes

RP1 (extract)

21 January 1894, Feast of St Agnes

On Sr Agnès's election as Prioress, Thérèse has been given the task of teaching the novices, nominally as assistant to Mère Marie de Gonzague, who has become Novice Mistress. The poems now become more frequent. Thérèse often used to compose them in her head during the day. She then did not put them on paper until the free time between Compline and Matins, and 'it was not without extreme difficulty that I remembered, at eight in the evening, what I had composed in the morning.' (*Conseils et Souvenirs*)

This poem is from Thérèse's first play, *The Mission of Joan of Arc, or The Shepherdess of Domrémy hearing her Voices*: see Translator's Introduction, page XXXIV. There are obvious parallels to Thérèse entering Carmel. She leaves her father, still at Les Buissonnets, and goes to war, to a voluntary and loving martyrdom.

---

l. 10 Lit. 'Must soon ring out, from the very heart of the battle.'

★ 'Master' ('to suffer for Love of You, O Master', in the preceding line) is P's word.

3

THE MELODY OF SAINT CECILIA

All the time the instruments were playing,
Cecilia was singing in her heart . . .
(Office of the Church)

O Saint I love so much, ' with joy I contemplate
That shining path-of-light ' which always stays with you:
I think I'm hearing still ' your melody! . . . ah, straight
From Heav'n your harmonies ' come down to me anew.
I'm still in exile, so ' to you my prayers are raised:
Oh, let me take my rest ' on your pure heart. For here
That spotless lily shone ' – on earth its splendour blazed:
So marvellous a flower ' had hardly any peer.

9   When suitors called, not one, ' Chaste Dove, did you admit –
For Jesus was the Love ' that you were wedded to:
He chose your soul, and to ' Himself united it;
Such virtues did He find ' – such fragrances in you! . . .
One mortal – youth ashine – ' he, too (to your distress)
Had breathed your perfume in, ' O heav'nly flower of white;
He sought to gather you ' – to gain your tenderness:
Valerian, who brought ' his heart, with love alight.
And, soon, he had prepared ' a sumptuous wedding-feast
And singers through the halls ' of all his palace sang:
Yet, in your maiden heart ' another song increased
Whose echo was divine ' and up to Heaven rang.
What *could* you sing – so far ' away your Home on high! –
In seeing, near to you, ' such mortal frailty?
Undoubtedly you wished, ' Cecilia, to die –
For Jesus, to be one ' with Him, eternally.

But no! I hear your lyre ' – angelic vibrances! –
The music of your love ' so sweetly it avows,
You raised up to the Lord ' that song whose words were this:
'Oh, keep me virgin-pure ' for You, my tender Spouse.'
Surrender (words all fail) ' – Divine the melody!
In that celestial hymn ' was love made manifest:
Such love as *does not fear*, ' forgetting all, to be
Upon the Heart of God ' a little child at rest . . .

33   So, to the vault of blue ' in purity there sailed
(To come and light it up) ' a white – a timid star . . .
Illumining the night, ' whose splendour was unveiled –
Thus, for this virgin pair, ' celestial glories are! . . .

Valerian dreamt, first, ' of earthly pleasure – for
Your love, Cecilia, ' was all that he desired –
And yet, in wedding you, ' discovered so much more;
In him, a love of Life ' Eternal you inspired!
'Young friend,' you said to him, ' 'near me – he never sleeps –
Here always, as a guard ' of my virginity,
An Angel of the Lord ' unending vigil keeps,
In joy, as with his wings ' of blue he covers me!
At night I see him – oh, ' his features then appear
More radiant than are ' the fires of dawn; for he
Is all a gentle flame: ' such purity is here,
The Face of God shines out ' of his transparency.'
Valerian replied, ' 'This angel *show* to me,
And then I might add Faith ' to this my pledge to you:
But tremble otherwise ' – for, look at me, and see
The fury, and the hate ' my love may turn into!'

[9]

O Dove inside the rock, ' you're hidden there, you can
Be safe! you needn't dread ' the hunter and his snare.
The Face of Jesus gives ' you light. Valerian
Now reads your heart and finds ' the Holy Gospel there . . .
Your answer came at once; ' you smiled as you replied:
'Yes, you will see him, soon, ' my Guardian! He'll come
To talk to you and tell ' you all that will betide –
To soar to Heav'n you first ' must face *your martyrdom!*
Before you see him, though, ' your Baptism – you need
Your soul to be made white ' by water; that is when
The True and Only God ' will live in you indeed!
The Holy Spirit . . . He ' will animate you then.
The Word – the Son of God, ' the Son of Mary too –
With love that is immense ' is on our altars here
As Sacrifice! The Bread ' of Heav'n is offered you:
To banquet, thus, on Life, ' Valerian, draw near!
The Seraph in the height ' will call you 'brother' – for
He sees his God enthroned ' in you, and will desire
To raise you from the earth, ' the ocean; he will draw
You up to where he dwells, ' this ardency of fire.'
'My heart is now aflame: ' a new felicity
(The nobleman exclaims) ' has caught it and it soars!
For, now, this Lord and God ' I want to live in me:
Cecilia! *my* love ' will be no less than yours.'

When, afterwards, the Robe ' of Innocence he wore
Valerian could see ' the shining angel. Now
He gazed upon the strength ' and loveliness he saw,
Delighting in the rays ' from that angelic brow.
The Seraph, as he shone ' held roses, and their red
Had there, along with them, ' a lily-burst of white.
(These blossoms opened up ' in Heaven's flower-bed,
Beneath the rays of Love ' of God's creative Light.)

'Dear heav'nly spouses! Crowns ' of Roses, soon, will ring
Your brows,' the Angel said; ' 'There are no words for this –
No voice, nor any lyre ' whose cadences can sing
Of martyrdom – of how ' immense a grace it is!
I cannot suffer so ' – though we, the Seraphim,
Are plunged in the abyss ' of God's own Beauty. I
Can never give Him tears, ' nor give, as you to Him
My blood, to *show* my love ' – for, oh! I cannot die.
Though *we* have purity ' as our angelic lot
(Our joy will never end) ' – though that is wholly true,
Compared with us, a great ' advantage you have got:
96 For you can both be pure ' and suffer for Him too!
. . . . . .

'Virginity's the state ' these lilies symbolize
(The Lamb has sent you them) ' . . . so fragrant will you be!
An aureole of white ' your glory signifies –
A song that's wholly new ' you'll sing, eternally!
Your union, so chaste, ' yet many souls will bear
Who Him as their true love, ' Him only, have professed:
You'll see them shine in Heav'n ' like flames of loving there,
Before the throne of God, ' the heart-home of the Blest.'

Lend me, Cecilia! ' your melody. Anew
I'd make a crowd of hearts ' love Jesus as they should;
Would immolate my life ' – completely, as did you,
Would offer Him as gifts ' my weeping and my blood.
Obtain for me the taste ' of perfect sacrifice –
Surrender – Fruit of Love ' upon this foreign shore.
Obtain for me, dear Saint, ' that, soon, my soul may rise
To Heaven, where I'll be ' near you, for evermore.

[11]

Notes

PN 3

28 April 1894 (Céline's twenty-fifth birthday)

' . . . alas, it would need another tongue than that of earth to express the beauty of the *abandon* [self-surrender] of a soul in the hands of Jesus . . . *Céline*, the story of *Cecilia* (*the Saint of* ABANDON) is your story too!' (Letter from Thérèse, 26 April 1894).

Thérèse wrote this poem for her sister, Céline, then looking after their sick father. With her thoughts on the future, she wanted to direct Céline's mind towards consecrated virginity, 'fruitful loss' as she called it in Poem 17. (But Thérèse said of her parents, whose holiness flowered in matrimony: 'God gave me a mother and father more worthy of heaven than of earth.')

Cecilia is an historical figure, a Roman martyr, probably of the late second/early third century. But the *Acts of the Martyrdom of St Cecilia*, which gives the legend on which Thérèse based her poem, is a 'pious romance' of the fifth century.

---

ll. 9–10 Lit., 'In going through life, you never sought any other spouse but Jesus'.

ll. 33–36 These four lines represent Cecilia dreaming, asleep like a child 'upon the Heart of her God'. The key lines on *abandon* are 31–32.

l. 36 Lit., 'The virginal love of the spouses in Heaven.'

l. 96 The dots between this and the next line come from Thérèse (seemingly to indicate transition to a different idea). Nothing has been omitted.

[4]

HYMN TO OBTAIN THE CANONIZATION OF THE VENERABLE JOAN OF ARC

1   O God of Hosts, the Church – the whole of us
     Would like, upon the Altar soon, to sing
     Of Maid, of Martyr; she the Valorous!
     Her praises through the courts of Heaven ring.

Refrain 1
O King! Advance
Your Maid's renown:
And give to Joan of France
The Altar and the Crown!

2   To conquer? No: to save the guilty France
     (None other could have); *that* she battled for.
     Let heroes – all, together! – take their stance,
     But still a martyr (such as she) weighs more!

3   For Joan is simply, Lord, Your work of art –
     What on this timid Maid did You endow?
     A warrior's soul You gave – a burning heart;
     Look: lilies now, and laurels, on her brow!

4   Joan, in a field heard Voices call, from Heav'n,
     They summoned her to battle: *'Go save France!'*
     She left, with this commission she'd been giv'n:
     And soldiers then were shaken by her glance!   ★[1]

5   She won the souls of haughty fighting-men –
       How pure the gaze of her, the Heaven-sent!
       She captured them with words of flame; and then
       Before her were audacious foreheads bent.

6   A marvel, this – unique in history:
       One sees a king who trembled with alarm
       And yet won back his crown . . . how can this be?
       He did it through a feeble child's right arm!

7   These are not, though, the victories of Joan
       That we have come today to celebrate –
       Because her *true* renown to us is known:
       Her purity! Her martyr's love was great.   ★²

8   Yes, Joan saved France, she led a holy war:
       But what had then her virtues to arouse?
       A seal of bitter suffering she bore,
       The blessed stamp of Jesus as her Spouse.

9   Joan gave up life – a high oblation, and
       Heard singing at the stake: because the Blest
       Drew up this exile to her Native Land.
       This Angel who'd saved France was now at rest!

10   Child warrior! – for you our hope remain –   ★³
       We beg you, hear us; from the height sublime
       Come down to us, convert our France again –
       Yes, come and save her for the second time!

May God advance
His arms! Our plea
Is that you'll save our France
Again, and make her free.

11 Daughter of God of Battles! ah, how tall
You were, in chasing out the Englishmen!
Remember, though, the days when you were small:
For feeble lambs were all you guarded then.

Refrain 3
Your warrior's arts
Use in defence,
Today, of children's hearts,
And of their innocence!

12 Sweet Martyr, you have *us*: the convent doors
Enclose your sisters, Joan. What is our rôle,
The object of our prayer? The same as yours –
We pray that God may reign in every soul.

Refrain 4
Give us – as seal
On our desire –
An Apostolic zeal,
O Joan! your Martyr's-fire.

13 Away from ev'ry heart will fear have flown
When we shall see the Church, our Mother, bring
The Saintly Crown to wreathe our lovely Joan! –
Then will it be that all of us can sing:

Refrain 5
Our hopes today
Are in your hands!
Then pray for us – O pray
For us, Saint Joan of France!

Notes

PN 4

8 May 1894

The above date, which Thérèse wrote on the manuscript of her poem, was a day of special celebration in Lisieux, as throughout France. Earlier that year Pope Leo XIII had authorized the introduction of the Cause of Beatification of Joan of Arc, thus according Joan the title 'Venerable' and permitting her to be honoured and prayed to publicly.

Pierre Cauchon, closely involved in the condemnation of Joan when Bishop of Beauvais, afterwards became Bishop of Lisieux. A later Bishop, Thomas Basin, was one of the promoters of Joan's rehabilitation in 1455–6.

On 8 May 1894, five thousand people crowded into the Cathedral of St Pierre at Lisieux. A 'rich standard of the glorious Liberatress' was placed in the chapel containing Cauchon's tomb. Céline, with other young people preparing for the occasion, had made 'twelve large white oriflammes scattered with fleurs-de-lys'.

St. 11, l. 1: 'how tall'. Thérèse wrote 'How beautiful were your steps', a phrase taken from Song of Songs 7:1.

★[1] 'shaken': from P's retouching, which stated that Joan's appearance alone (later editions; 1898, voice alone) 'shook' the soldiers. This was a more vigorous substitute for Th's perhaps ambiguous 'commanded' the army.

★[2] Th here wrote only of Joan's love and virtues in general.

★[3] 'Child' is P's. Th simply addressed Joan by name.

MY SONG OF TODAY

1   My life's a jot of time,
                    an hour that comes and goes;
     My life – this moment; *now* –
                    escapes and runs away.
     To give You while on earth,
                    O God, the love one owes,
            I've got . . . only today!

2   I love you, Jesus; *You*
                    this soul aspires to! I
     Wish – only for today –
                    my head on You to lay:
     Come, rule my heart, and smile
                    upon me in reply –
            This, but just for today!

3   What do I care, O Lord,
                    that darkness may pervade?
     Tomorrow – ah, for that
                    I simply cannot pray! . . .
     Oh, make my heart stay pure,
                    enwrap me in Your shade:
            This, but just for today.

4   Tomorrow? Dream of that
                and wavering I fear –
For then I feel a gloom,
                a boredom, on its way:
But trials do I want,
                O God, and suff'ring here;
        This I want, for today.

5   I *shall* behold You soon
                on that eternal shore,
O God, my Pilot! where
                I shall my anchor weigh:
My little boat, in peace,
                guide through the thunder-roar:
        This, but just for today.

6   Lord, let me hide myself –
                find refuge in your Face,
No longer hear the world
                and all its idle bray.
Ah! give to me your Love,
                stay by me with your grace –
        This, but just for today.

7   The nearness of your Heart
                forgetfulness ensures:
No more the Enemy   ★[1]
                can frighten or dismay.
O Jesus, grant a place
                inside that Heart of yours:
        This, but just for today.

8   O touching Mystery!   ★²
                    O Bread of Heaven's height!
       O Living Bread, of Love's
                    bestowal! come, I pray –
       Come, Jesus; live within
                    my heart, O Host of white! –
              This, but just for today.

9   O deign that You, the Vine
                    I'll stay united to:
       For You, this feeble branch
                    will all its fruit display;
       Then, harvest-grapes of gold
                    I can be off'ring You,
              Lord . . . from when? From today!

10   This harvest-gift of love –
                    with souls for grapes – must be
       Made up in just a day,
                    this day that flies away:
       A true Apostle's fire,
                    O Jesus, give to me! –
              This, but just for today.

11   O Spotless Virgin, you're
                    the star by which I sail!
       You light up Jesus; you   ★³
                    unite me with Him. May
       I rest, O Mother, in
                    the safety of your veil:
              This, but just for today.

12   My Guardian Angel, come
                    enfold me in your wing,
      Behold me, gentle friend –   ★⁴
                    light up for me the way.
      I call on you for help,
                    direct my journeying!
        This, but just for today.

13   I want to see my Lord
                    unveiled, uncloudedly;
      But, far from Him I pine,
                    in exile. So I say:
      'Oh, that You will not hide
                    your lovely Face from me!' –
        This, but just for today.

14   I soon shall fly to You,
                    to praise You, my Desire.
      When day without an end
                    sheds on my soul its ray,
      I shall be singing – to
                    the Holy Angels' lyre –
        That Eternal 'Today'!

Notes

PN 5

1 June 1894, Feast of the Sacred Heart of Jesus

'We have only the brief instant of life to *give* to the good God . . . and already He is preparing to say, "Now it's my turn . . ."' (Thérèse, letter to Céline, 19 August 1894).

This poem was written as a feast-day gift for her sister, Marie (Sr Marie of the Sacred Heart).

Metre The first syllable of each last line should be heavily stressed. This reproduces a first syllable of intensity in the French.

St. 2, l. 2 Lit. (addressed to Jesus): 'For one day only, stay (as) my gentle support.'

St. 4, l. 1 'wavering', i.e. inconstancy.

★¹ Th left unspecified those 'fears', in night hours, which she does not 'dread'. P specifies 'the features of the Enemy'.

★² 'touching' – an adjective in loving reaction to the Mystery – is P's.

★³ 'light up': P continues the metaphor of a star. Th wrote 'give me' Jesus.

★⁴ 'gentle friend' is P's and fills up the metre. Th's words, replaced by it, carried overtones of her *individual* road: one's spiritual journey is on the road one travels, not elsewhere.

[6]

PRAYER OF THE CHILD OF A SAINT

1   Recall that here on earth your happiness
       Lay in your looking after us! We pray
       That you who go on loving us, will bless
       Your children – will protect us still today.
   You've reached your Homeland, where
               you're met and greeted by
   Our mother dear – there, long
               before you, up on high:
               In Heaven now you reign
               Together. Both again,
                   Watch over us!

2   Recall Marie, that loving daughter who
       Was to your heart the dearest of us . . . yes,
       Recall, as well: she made life full for you
       With all her love and charm and happiness.
   God called her then, so – for
               His sake! – you didn't cling:
   Instead, you blessed the hand
               that offered Suffering.
               Your lovely 'Diamond' – oh,
               The one that sparkled so,
                   Remember now!

       And Pauline – she the 'Pearl of Beauty'! – too:
       At home, a weak and timid 'lamb' – but how
       God's strength has since possessed the one you knew;
       It's she who leads the flock of Carmel now!

Yes, she is Mother to
　　　　　your other children here –
Come, guide her here below,
　　　　　that one, to you so dear!
　　　　Still, from your place above,
　　　　Your little Carmel love! . . .
　　　　　　Remember now . . .

4　　　Your *third* child now recall, and all the prayer
　　　　You offered up to God, so ardently . . .
　　　　He heard! She knows the earth and all that's there
　　　　As exile for her spirit, Léonie.　　★[1]
The Visitation hides
　　　　　her from the world, but she
Loves Jesus; and His peace
　　　　　now floods her like a sea!
　　　　Recall, and hear the sighs –
　　　　Her ardent longings – rise,
　　　　　　Remember now!

5　　　Recall, your faithful Céline also: she
　　　　The angel who was taking care of you
　　　　(For then God's gaze had meant that you would be
　　　　Tried, by a choice so glorious – there too).
You reign in Heav'n . . . her task
　　　　　is finished. By her vow
Her life is given up
　　　　　to Jesus wholly now.
　　　　Protect her, we entreat,
　　　　The one you hear repeat,
　　　　　　'Recall me now!'.

6   Remember, too, your 'Little Queen': you know
How lavish all her tendernesses were! ★[2]
Recall: her little footsteps faltered so –
Your hand it was that always guided her.
Papa, you wished your child
         to keep her childhood: hence
You sought (for God alone)
        to guard her innocence . . .
    Her locks of gold – a sight
    That gave you such delight –
       Recall them now!

7   And often, too, up in the belvedere
You'd take her on your knee, and you would bring
Contentment to her with a prayer . . . she'd hear
The gentle cradle-song that you would sing.
What she would see was Heav'n
        reflected in your face
When, there, your gaze was drawn
        profoundly into space.
    Song . . . of *Eternity*:
    The Beauty there would be! –
      Recall that now.

8   One Sunday – how that day was full of light –
You pressed her to your heart, a father . . . you,
In giving her a little flower of white,
Agreed that *she* could fly to Carmel too!
Papa! Your love – which bore
        such heavy trials here –
Gave proof to her, by that,
        that it was most sincere!
    At Bayeux, and at Rome,
    You showed her Heav'n – her Home! –
      Recall that now.

9   Recall we saw the Holy Father's hand
             Rest on your forehead. Yet there was concealed
             One mystery! . . . you couldn't understand
             The print of God by which your brow was sealed.
     Your children bless the cross,
                  your bitter sorrow – how
     You suffered then! But they
                    are praying to you now.
               Your forehead bears a sign,
               In Heav'n! . . . in rays that shine,
                  Nine lilies flower!!!

Notes

PN 8

August 1894

'. . . the holy patriarch who has delighted Heaven by his fidelity' (Thérèse, letter to Céline, 6 July 1893).

Thérèse's father, Louis Martin, died on 29 July 1894. He had suffered, from 1887 onwards, a series of strokes, which had been followed by some disorder of mind. The death of Louis meant that it would now be possible for Céline to enter Carmel, if a fourth Martin sister were accepted there.

From Thérèse's knowledge of Louis' holiness – and because an event which she audaciously told God would be a sign from Heaven immediately took place – Thérèse was certain that Louis had gone straight to God: hence the title of the poem.

Louis, and his wife Zélie, Thérèse's mother (d. 1877), were declared 'Venerable' on 26 March 1994: a step in their joint beatification cause.

St. 2, l. 7 'Diamond': Louis's pet name for Marie.

St. 3, ll. 1–2 'Pearl of Beauty'/'lamb': 'Real pearl' (*perle fine*) and 'lamb' were Louis' pet names for Pauline.

St. 4, l. 5 'The Visitation': the Visitation Convent at Caen.

St. 5, ll. 3–4 'glorious choice', i.e. choice by God, in relation to Louis' suffering. In *Aut.* (Ms. A) Thérèse, in referring to her father's illness, describes it as a 'glorious trial'.

St. 6, l. 1 'Little Queen': Louis' pet name for Thérèse herself, much quoted by Thérèse (*Aut.*, Ms. A) in describing her life at Les Buissonnets, the family home in Lisieux.

St. 9, l. 9 'Nine lilies' A little after her father's death, Thérèse made and decorated a chasuble from a gown of her mother's. The design, within a cross, was of the Holy Face together with two white roses (her parents), four lily buds (her brothers and sisters who died in infancy) and five lilies (her sisters and herself).

★[1] Th's wording described Léonie and the other four Martins as *lilies*. P deleted this, perhaps because she modestly objected to herself being thus described so explicitly. Th, who included *her*self, would surely have ascribed all the brilliance of that 'lily' to God.

★[2] This retouched line is P describing Th. Th simply included another of the pet names her father called her.

7

THE STORY OF A SHEPHERDESS
BECOME QUEEN

Written for the Profession Day
of Sr Marie-Madeleine

1   We've come to sing, O Madeleine,
This lovely day you make your vows,
About the marvel of that chain
Which gently binds you to your Spouse!
Hear now the charming story: Once
A shepherdess became the choice,
The loved one, of a King! . . . she runs
Toward him when she hears his voice.

      Refrain
   This shepherdess sing:
   Since Heaven's High King –
   She, here, being poor –
Will marry her! – now, evermore.

2   Look at this little shepherd-girl! –
She guards her lambs, and spins, as she
Sees how the flower-buds unfurl,
Delights in birdsong from the tree;
Attuned to what all things declare
In those great woods and that blue sky . . .
For everything of goodness there
Revealed to her her God on high.

3   She loving *them* so ardently,
     Jesus and Mary, to impart
     Proof of their love for Mélanie,
     Talked to her one day, heart to heart.
     'Will you,' the Gentle Queen invites,
     'Live near me, and for name be giv'n
     "Madeleine"? There, on Carmel's heights,
     You will gain nothing else than *Heav'n*!

4   'Child, leave here, with light heart, and count
     Your flock no longer!: now I am
     Calling you to my sacred mount,
     Jesus will be your only Lamb!'
     'Oh! come, your soul has captured me,'
     Repeated Jesus, 'for I vow
     I take you for my bride-to-be,
     You will be mine for ever, now!'

5   Hearing, the shepherdess at once
     In joy, sets out and will not stop;
     Led by her Mother, Mary – runs
     And climbs Mount Carmel to the top.
     . . . . . .
     You, little Madeleine, we mean!
     Of *you*, on this great day, we sing:
     A Shepherdess become a Queen –
     Jesus's Love, and He your King!

6   My dearest Sister, this you know:
     To serve our God – *that* is to reign!
     The Gentle Saviour, here below,
     Throughout His teaching made this plain:
     'Your aim is that in Heaven you

Shall have all other souls surpassed?
Then *this*, life-long, you'll have to do –
Hide yourself, wholly . . . be the last!'

7   O happy Madeleine! you're at
     Your place in Carmel, where your prayer
     To Jesus . . . *could* one toil in that,
     Being so close to Heaven there?
     Martha and Mary, both! – for you
     Pray to and serve your Saviour – yes,
     This end you always have in view;
     It gives you your true happiness.

8   If sometimes bitter suffering
     Has come to you, to be a guest
     Make it your joy, that bitter thing –
     Suff'ring for God is sweet and blest.
     Divine caresses thereupon
     Will make you, soon, forget you tread
     Those jagged thorns you're walking on –
     You'll think you're flying then, instead!

9   The Angels envy you, and they,
     Seeing your happiness, are awed
     At that which you possess today –
     Being the spouse, now, of the Lord!
     The holy angels all adore   ★[1]
     That King who's chosen you as bride:
     Singing His praises evermore,
     You'll soon be reigning, by His side.

Last refrain
Soon will – Heav'n her gain –
The shepherdess reign
(She, here, being poor)
By the side of God, evermore!   ★²

Notes

PN 10

20 November 1894

'. . . behold, thy time was the time of lovers: and I spread my garment over thee . . . saith the Lord God: and thou becamest mine . . . I clothed thee with embroidery . . . and put . . . a chain about thy neck . . . thou . . . wast made exceeding beautiful: and wast advanced to be a queen' (Ezekiel 16: 8–13), quoted by Thérèse in Ms. A: 'God accomplished for me what Ezekiel reports in his prophecies'.

Sr Marie-Madeleine (Mélanie Lebon), a lay sister strikingly handsome of feature, had been a shepherdess in actual fact. As a novice, she herself wrote, she 'was not in a state to profit from' Thérèse's advice, 'but after (Thérèse's) entry into heaven, I surrendered to her the care of my soul, and how she changed me! It's unbelievable! . . . I don't recognize myself any more.' Her testimony to the diocesan tribunal is frank and moving.

St. 5 The dots are Thérèse's; nothing has been omitted.
★¹ P recast the second half of the stanza, omitting Th's emphasis that Marie-Madeleine was a 'spouse' already (and not only later, in heaven).
★² Th added a stanza and refrain in which the Reverend Mothers of the Carmel were thanked for their part in Marie-Madeleine's vocation. P deleted this: she was amongst the Reverend Mothers thanked!

8

THE QUEEN OF HEAVEN, TO HER WELL-LOVED CHILD, MARIE

'Marie of the Holy Face' was the name as a postulant of Thérèse's sister, Céline. She later became Sr Geneviève.

1   A little child I'm seeking, who's
     Like Jesus . . . this I want to do –
     To hide her, with my Lamb: I'll use   ★
     Only one cradle for the two.

2   Though Angels feel a jealousy
     That joys as great as yours arouse,
     I'll nonetheless give you, Marie,
     The Holy Child to be your Spouse! . . .

3   I sought a child I wished to be
     Jesus's sister . . . *you* I chose.
     Will you, then, keep Him company?
     My heart is here for your repose.

4   I'll hide and cradle you (this veil
     Enfolds the King of Heaven too):
     My glorious Son will never fail
     To be the bright daystar for you.

5   But, shelter always? That you may
     Under my veil with Jesus hide,
     A little thing you'll have to stay,
     By childhood virtues beautified.

6   Though wanting you to radiate
        Both gentleness and purity,
        What most I give, to animate
        Your spirit, is simplicity.

7   The great God – One, in Persons three;
        The angels tremble at His power,
        Eternal One ! – wants just to be,
        To you, as though a meadow-flower . . .

8   The simple daisy, open-eyed,
        Looks upward on its slender stem:
        You be a sister-flower beside
        The little Babe of Bethlehem!

9   His charms – a King in exile, He –
        The world still fails to recognize:
        And, often, tears of grief you'll see
        Glistening in His baby eyes.

10   Forget (you must!) your weariness,
        To make this lovely Child rejoice:
        Your chains – so gentle! – you should bless,
        Gently and with a lilting voice.

11   Great God, who causes billows wild
        To hush – what did You come to seek?
        To make Yourself a little child! –
        For us, becoming small and weak.

12   The Uncreated Word, to be
        Your little Brother! and my Son!
        An exile here . . . for you, Marie:
        What words now will He utter? None!

13   Let silence speak – as token, and
Unutterable love convey:
God's wordless speech you'll understand,
You'll imitate it every day.

14   If sometimes Jesus sleeps, you will
Stay in repose, besides Him, too! –
His Heart (at watch, though He is still)
In gentleness, supporting you.

15   Don't worry about work, Marie,
For what your daily labour tells
Is how you love (for this should be
Your work – *all love*, and nothing else).

16   If someone comes along and says
'You work, but what have you to show?',
'I love, and much, so I possess'
You say, 'such *riches*, here below!'

17   With bays will Jesus wreathe your brow,
If you want nothing but His love:
If you're surrendered to Him now,
You'll reign, one day, with Him above!

18   You'll see Him gaze at you – the night
Will be ablaze that once was black!
You'll fly to Heav'n, in high delight,
With nothing now to hold you back!

Notes

PN 13

25 December 1894, a Christmas gift to Céline, placed in her shoe.

'Childhood, which in natural life is only a transitory state leading to adulthood, becomes, in the sphere of grace, the ideal state, the final flowering of the whole spiritual destiny. The Christian will no longer strive to pass beyond this new childhood but to tend toward it . . .' (Père Victor de la Vièrge, O.C.D. (Victor Sion), *Spiritual Realism of St Thérèse of Lisieux.*)

Early in the year which is about to begin, Thérèse's sister, Marie (Sr Marie of the Sacred Heart) will, by a simple question, cause Pauline (Mère Agnès) to order Thérèse to begin what became her autobiography: 'Is it possible that you should permit her to compose little poems to please everybody, and that she should write nothing for us about all the memories of her childhood?' (deposition to the diocesan tribunal).

★ P, 'hide'; Th, 'guard'.

[9]

TO SAINT JOSEPH

1 Though poverty of life you knew,
   Saint Joseph, there is this to say:
   At Jesus, and at Mary you
   Gazed . . . upon *beauty* every day.

   Refrain
   Most tender Joseph, haste –
   Protect our Carmel! Oh!
   Let all your children, always, taste
   The peace of Heaven, here below

2 The Son of God, in infancy,
   How often by your arms was pressed,
   As, meek to your authority,
   He found upon your heart His rest.

3 Jesus and Mary . . . yes! we, too –
   In solitude we serve them: for
   We work to please them, as did you;
   That's what we want on earth – no more!

4 Our Mother, Saint Teresa – who
   Confided in you always – stressed
   She found that when she prayed to you
   Quick answer came to each request.

5

And so . . . till Heav'n our trials here
Concludes . . . one joyous hope we share:
That – with our heav'nly Mother dear –
Saint Joseph, we shall see you there!

Last refrain
We, tender Father, call! –
Our little Carmel bless:
Our exile over, may we all
Unite, in Heaven's happiness!

Notes

PN 14

1894

'I thank you, Monsieur l'Abbé, for having chosen me as godmother of the first child you will have the joy of baptizing; it is, then, up to me to choose the names of my future godchild. I want to give it as protectors: the Blessed Virgin, St Joseph, and St Maurice . . .' (Thérèse, letter of 24 February 1897 to the Abbé Maurice Bellière: see note to Poem 34.)

––––––––––––––––––––

St. 4, l. 1 'Our Mother, Saint Teresa': St Teresa of Avila.

Poems 10 to 15 are extracts from Thérèse's play
Joan of Arc accomplishing her mission.

[10]

JOAN'S HYMN AFTER
HER VICTORIES

1 All, all! to You, Almighty, be
The glory of the battle-sword
(Since victory was *given* me! –
A child so weak and timid, Lord.)
And oh, my Mother Mary! you,
A guiding planet, always bright –
Your shining in my path, I knew,
Protected me, from Heaven's height.
When shall I go (from waiting here,
Sweet star, whose gentle splendour shined!)
To see that blazing whiteness, clear? –
And, underneath your veil, to find
  Your heart a place of rest for me.

2 Earth's joys can not content my soul;
It wants Eternal Happiness!
It feels its exile here: its goal
Is God in Heav'n – and *nothing less.*
This, too, I want (before I go
To see my Jesus in His Light):
To win Him countless souls, and so
To love Him more and more. To fight!
And soon, to that celestial shore
(My exile like a single day)
I'll fly, and there, for evermore, ★
All cloud, all shadow, rolled away . . .
  My Love, my *Jesus,* I shall see!

Notes

RP 3 (extract)

21 January 1895

'For my mission, like that of Joan of Arc, "the will of God will be accomplished in spite of the jealousy of men"' (Thérèse, on her deathbed, to Pauline).

St. 1. l. 4 'A child so weak...' 'When Thérèse speaks of herself as little, it is not a childish complacency but an objective view of her relationship with God. If He is All, she is nothing without Him; nevertheless, she can do all things with His grace' (Père Victor de la Vièrge, O.C.D., *op. cit.*)

★ 'for evermore': Th's words were, 'He will embrace me' for ever.

JOAN'S PRAYER IN PRISON

1 My Voices told of this: ' in prison I am thrown –
   I have no hope of aid, ' except, O God, from You!
   I left my father – and ' he's old – for You alone:
   I left the flowered fields, ' the sky, unchanging blue.
   I left my dear Mama, ' my valley, and I came ★
   And showed to those who fought ' the standard of the Cross:
   For, Lord, the army I ' commanded in Your name!
   And generals – no less – ' attended to my voice.

2 And now! – a prison cell ' the wages that were due?
   For work and tears, and blood, ' this recompense is mine!
   I shall not see again ' the places that I knew,
   The smiling countryside ' where meadow-flowers twine;
   I shall not see again, ' afar, the mountain-top –
   Its snow, that in the blue ' dipped white, as though a wave.
   And never shall I hear ' the chiming start and stop,
   The bell which in clear air ' its dreamy summons gave . . .

3 That star I seek in vain, ' shut up in this dim jail,
   Which, sparkling in the sky, ' would ev'ning vigil keep,
   The leaves, that in the Spring ' would serve me as a veil
   (I'd try to guard the flock ' but then would fall asleep!).
   When, now, between these tears, ' my senses melt away
   I dream about the vale, ' its charm of bush and tree,
   The freshness of the dawn, ' the scent of early day:
   But then! . . . the clank of chains ' awakes me, suddenly.
   . . . . . .

4   My martyrdom! and I ˈ accept it, for Your love;
          No more do I fear death ˈ or dread the burning fire:
          For, Jesus, how my soul ˈ sighs now for You above –
          Aspires to You alone, ˈ my God, and my Desire!
          I want to take my cross ˈ and follow You, to give
          My life for love of You, ˈ sweet Saviour. This is why
          I have a sole desire ˈ – that I begin to live!
          That He and I be one ˈ is why I want to die.

Notes

The dots between the third and fourth stanzas indicate omission of prose
and verse. The poem is here given as in *Histoire d'une Ame*.

St. 1, l. 3 'for You alone': lit., 'for Your love alone'.

★ P inserted the reference to Joan's mother, thus weakening the parallel
   with Th herself, for it was their father only whom Th left behind at Les
   Buissonnets (Zélie, their mother, having died when Th was 4½).

12

JOAN'S VOICES DURING
HER MARTYRDOM

1   From the Eternal Country we come down,
     To smile at you; you come to Heaven now:
     See, in our hands, your high immortal crown,
     To shine – a blaze of glory – on your brow!

2   Come with us, then, O Maid so dear,
          To radiant firmaments of blue;
          Come Home! No more your exile here! –
               Life, in our joyous sphere:
                    God's daughter, you.

. . . . . .

3   The stake is lit! God's Love, however – for
     It *also* is a Flame – it rises higher!
     Eternal Dew – ah! simply minutes more –
     Will come to quench the torture of the fire.

4   Deliverance! The swaying bough,
          The martyr's palm, is waiting you:
          See (angel, liberator!) how
               Jesus comes to you now! –
                    'Greatheart' and true.

5   Dear Martyr-Maid, a second and no more,
     Your suffering, and then eternal rest.
     Weep not! – your death is saving France! You'll draw   ★
     Her children up, to live among the Blest.

Joan sings:

6

> I enter Life, and, as I go,
> See saints and angels, there Above!
> I die to save my country so . . .
>> Come to me, Mary – oh,
>> Jesus, my Love!

Notes

The dots between the second and third stanzas indicate the omission of a short passage of prose.

_____

★ 'Weep not!' is P's.

13

JOAN: THE DIVINE JUDGMENT

1   I hear your voice on high –
                 I answer you, my love:
And now I break your bonds,
                 unloosen ev'ry chain!
Fly swiftly up to me,
                 my fair and beauteous dove –
For winter now is gone:
                 in Heaven, *come and reign*!
      Yes, I your Judge decree it, Joan;
      Your Angel claims you as his own,
      And I – I make my judgment known:
I've seen you shining with the flame of love!

2   So come, it is your Crowning-day! –
      Your tears I want to dry by this:
      Your exile's night has gone away –
      Oh, come to Me, receive my kiss!

3   Mount higher, above –
        Companioned! Move
        Through meadows, my love,
        The Lamb drawing you:

4   Oh, come to my side
        (You, chosen as bride) –
        To sing, glorified,   ★
        Your song that is new . . .

5   (They laud you, in Light,
           The phalanx of white –
           The Angels unite
           Melodiously) . . .

6   Meek shepherdess, who
           Are warrior, too –
           Earth's honour of you
           Unended shall be!
           Meek shepherdess, who
           Are warrior – you
           Have *Heaven* from Me!

Notes

St. 1, l. 8 'I've seen you shining . . .' This unrhymed line is unrhymed in the French.

★ 'glorified' (*transformée*) is P's, but is wholly consistent with Th's thought – which P, one may say, brought out.

14

JOAN IN HEAVEN:
THE CANTICLE OF TRIUMPH

1   *The Saints address Joan*:
            This crown is yours, and for eternity:
This Martyr's-palm is yours,
                        as well; and now we bring
The throne we have prepared,   ★[1]
                        resplendent. It will be
            Near to the King.

2   Ah, in the heavens here,
                        pure singing-dove, remain –
For ever you've escaped
                        the hunters and the snare.
You'll find the little brook
                        that murmurs on the plain:
            Wide meadows, and the flowers there.

3   Then, dove, take wing: on pinions of white,
Each high and golden star
                        you can be visiting!
To Heav'n's aethereal vaults
                        unending, rise in flight –
            O dove, take wing!

4   No enemies *now*, Joan! –
                    No prison dark is yours.
The Seraph, as he shines,
                  knows you as sister fair!
See what your Love and Lord
                to you, His spouse, assures –
You, ever, on His Heart He'll bear.

                Joan:
5   Ah, He is mine! . . . sweet, that, beyond compare.
All Heaven now is mine!

               The Saints:
      All Heaven thine, we sing!

                Joan:
All! Mary, angels, saints –
              and God Himself! I'm heir
To Everything!

Note

★ P's retouching has the throne prepared by the Saints; Th's wording had it prepared by the Lord of Hosts, Himself.

15

PRAYER OF FRANCE
TO JOAN OF ARC

France, personified, speaks.

1   Remember, Joan, the country of your birth –
The flower-coloured valleys, and recall
The fields that seemed exuberant with mirth:
To go and wipe my tears, you left it all!
Remember also, Joan,
           that, angel-like and pure,
You saw your France was sick,
           and came to bring the cure:
Your France, today – oh, hark! –
Is groaning in the dark:
          'Recall that now!'

2   Recall the shining victories you'd win –
Orleans and then Reims would shower thanks.
Recall that you made glorious, and in
The name of God, the kingdom of the Franks.
But now, so far from you,
          I suffer and I sigh;
'Come, save me, once again,
          sweet martyr, Joan!', I cry:
Shear through these irons so:
The wrongs I've suffered – oh,
          Remember now.

. . . . . .

3   I come to you: with chains my arms are bound,
       A veil is hiding eyes that weepings mar:
       In sorrows of my children I am drowned –
       Not now among the greatest queens there are!
   God's nothing to them now;
               their Mother they neglect –
   Your pity, to my woes –
               so bitter, Joan! direct:
           Return, 'Greatheart'! Advance
           And save us! . . . for your France
               Hopes in you now.

Note

The dots between the second and third stanzas indicate a passage of verse, omitted from *Histoire d'une Ame*, in which Joan in heaven encourages France's approach to her.

16

SONG OF THANKS OF
JESUS'S BETROTHED

*Written for the day of Céline's clothing
in the habit of Carmel.*

1   You've hidden me, O Jesus, in Your Face . . . ★[1]
    My God and Friend! Oh, hear me as I sing ★[2]
    Of what is inexpressibly the grace
    Of carrying the Cross . . . of Suffering.

2   For long I've drunk a draught of tears, like You,
    I've shared Your cup of sorrows: yet in this
    That suffering has charms my heart knows too;
    One can save sinners – through the Cross, this is!

3   The Cross! by which my soul has grown in grace
    And light to see a new horizon by:
    Beneath the incandescence of Your Face
    My feeble heart, by You, is lifted high.

4   My Love, Your gentle voice is calling me;
    I hear Your 'Come, already Winter's gone!
    For you, my bride, the Spring begins to be.
    Night has at last its end. Behold the Sun!

5   'Lift up your eyes, and see your Homeland! Here
    You'll find – upon their thrones and honoured so –
    A tender Father, and a Mother dear:
    Huge happiness like yours, to them you owe!

6   'Your life, a trice, will melt away, like dew –
Heaven, to Carmel's heights, is very near:
Oh, dry your tears; my Heart has chosen you   ★³
For an eternal fire of loving here!'   ★⁴

Notes

PN 16

5 February 1895

'Let us not refuse Him the least sacrifice. Everything is so big in religion . . .
Picking up a pin through love can convert a soul! What a mystery!'
(Thérèse, letter to Léonie, 22 May 1894.)

★¹ 'hidden': Th added 'for ever', *pour toujours*. P, therefore, omitted a
thought which was at the depths of Th's spirituality: that of God's love
for her *being faithful and without recall* ('sans retour' is a common
phrase of Th's to describe her love for God also).

★² 'friend' is P's addition here (but it is a Theresian word).

★³ 'dry your tears' is P's.

★⁴ This wording is P's. Th's wording suggested a royal court in heaven.

17

LIVING BY LOVE!

1   List'ning in Love's hushed Evening, you'd have heard
Jesus say plainly: 'He who would love Me,
Let him be true, let him obey my Word:
Father and Son his Visitants shall be.
Our palace there, his heart a dwelling-place,   ★¹
An heir to peace and happiness above;
Our will it is that he forever stays –
     In our own Love.'

2   Living by Love . . . means guarding you – ah, You
The uncreated Word, the Holy Name!
Jesus, I love You. You – God – know I do,
Love's Spirit sets me blazing with His flame.
My love of *You* attracts the Father – oh,
My feeble heart forbids Him to get free!
O Trinity – a Prisoner! as so
     Love-locked by me.

3   *To live* is by Your life and lovingly:
King, and the bright delight of Heaven's day,
Hidden as Wafer here, You live for me:
Jesus, for You I'll also hide away!
Lovers – by night, by day – need solitude,
The heart-to-heart which only it can give.
Your glance alone gives me beatitude –
     By Love I live!

4 Living by Love . . . that means: don't pitch one's tent
On Thabor's summit when upon this earth,
But climb another hill where Jesus went;
Go with Him – know the Cross of priceless worth.
In Heav'n I have to shout aloud and sing –
For then no more one's love one needs to prove.
In Carmel, *this* I want: in suffering
  Living by Love.

5 Living by Love means 'Give unendingly,
Claiming no earthly wage!'. I do not doubt
This . . . I have stopped all counting up. I see
That when one loves, one doesn't measure out!
All, to the heart of God (whose tenderness
Spills over!) I have given. And, that done,
Light – but my riches in me – on I press;
  Lovingly run.

6 Living by Love means banishing all fear –
All glancing-back to faults of earlier day:
Of my past sins I see no imprint here,
Love in a trice has burnt them all away!
O Sacred Fire! O Furnace-flames' caress!
Here, in your home, I stay and will not move;
Singing, by your hearth-blaze in restfulness:
  'I live by Love!' . . .

7 Living by Love . . . 'Guard – in oneself, I mean –
One mighty Treasure in a mortal vase.'
Dear Love! I'm weak – as weak as ever seen;
I'm far from being an angel in the stars! . . .
But, if I fall in all the hours that go
You lift me ev'ry time, and I receive
Grace, ev'ry passing second from You, so
  By Love I live.

8   Living by Love means 'Set unbroken course
In spreading peace and joy to all in view.'
Dear Pilot! Charity's my driving-force:
In souls – my sisters – I am seeing You.
Charity . . . only star by which I sail –
On, by its light, undeviating move . . .
I've my device inscribed upon my veil:
     'Living by Love.'

9   Living by Love means too: while Jesus sleeps,
Staying reposeful when rough waters roar.
Don't fear I'll wake you up, Lord: on the deeps,
Tranquil I'll wait to reach the Heavenly shore . . . .
Soon Faith will take and tear apart her veil,
My Hope . . . a day, and then to You I fly:
Charity swells my veil out, like a sail –
     By Love, live I!

10   Living by Love means . . . Master! to implore
You spread Your Fires in priestly souls. For him,
Your chosen, holy Priest – let him be more
Pure in his spirit than the seraphim.
Glory upon your Deathless Church confer,
I beg You ev'ry moment, as I cry:
'Her child, I immolate myself for her:
     Love, I live by.'

11   Living by Love – the wiping of your Face,
That sinners of their weight of sin be rid:
O God of Love! may they return to grace
And bless your Name as ne'er before they did . . .
Blasphemy strikes my heart, I hear it still;
To blot it out, I'll sing for evermore
'Your Name, your Sacred Name, I always will
     Love and adore!'

12 Living by Love – it's like the Magdalene
  Bathing, with tears and precious perfumes there
  Your feet divine, with joyous kiss, and seen
  Wiping them gently with her flowing hair . . . .
  And, rising up, she breaks the vase. In turn
  Your gentle Face she now embalms from this:
  My perfume, for embalming, then discern –
    My Love it is!

13 'Living by Love – what folly, how bizarre!'
  So says the world. 'Stop singing,' it will say;
  'Don't lose your life, your perfumes as they are –
  Learn how to use them in the proper way!'
  Loving You, Jesus – *loss*? But fruitful so!
  My perfumes are for You alone, that's why –
  All. And I'll sing, as from this world I go:
    'Of Love I die!'

14 Dying of Love . . . so sweet a martyrdom –
  To that I hope my suff'rings will extend:
  Cherubim, tune your lyre for what's to come –
  For this I sense: my exile's going to end!
  Love's fire! consume me ruthlessly; I seem,
  Living at all, so burdened as I cry:
  'Jesus, my God! oh, realize my dream –
    Of Love to die!'

15 Dying of Love! Behold my hope, when hence
  I go, and see my bonds are broken: when
  My God will be my Mighty Recompense –
  I'm looking for no other Fortune then.
  I'm longing for His Love – and oh! that He
  Will come at last, consuming me above ★²
  Always. Behold my Heav'n, my destiny:
    Living by Love!!!

Notes

PN 17

26 February 1895

In the French, Thérèse's poetical masterpiece. It has been described as 'a "catechesis" of love', 'rich, profound and large'.

'. . . I wrote from memory, during my evening silence, the fifteen stanzas I had composed . . . during the day . . .' (*Last Conversations*, 5 August 1897).

'. . . a bit of verse for which I would willingly barter all the poetry of France': the Abbé Combes, of 'O Trinity! you are the prisoner of my love!' in stanza 2 (address delivered in the Lisieux Carmel, 30th September 1947).

St. 2, l. 2 'the Holy Name': Thérèse in fact wrote 'Parole de mon Dieu'.

St. 3, l. 1 Thérèse, in writing 'vivre de ta vie', alludes to the thought expressed by St Paul: 'And I live, now not I, but Christ liveth in me' (Gal. 2:20).

St. 3, l. 2 Lit., 'Glorious King, delight of the elect.'

St. 4, l. 5 'shout aloud and sing' Lit., 'live a life of enjoyment' (*vivre de jouissance*).

St. 12, l. 5 '. . . what does it matter that our vases be broken . . .?' (Thérèse, letter to Céline, 19 August 1894.)

★¹ 'palace' is P's; but the word is Theresian.

★² 'consuming'. In addition to this metaphor *of fire*, Th wrote of seeing, and being united with, God.

18

WHAT I LOVED . . .

The Canticle of Céline

1
    Oh, how I love the memory
    Of blessèd days in infancy –
My innocence a flower He guarded . . . He
    Surrounded me, the Lord above
      With love!

2
    Yes, I was little: nonetheless
    My heart was filled with tenderness –
This love it had, it could not but express:
    My promise to the King of Heav'n
      Was giv'n!

3
    Through springtime, still, how dear to me
    Would Mary and St Joseph be!
I'd plunge in rapturous as in a sea:
    My eyes caught Heaven's blue – no slight
      Delight!

4
    I loved the plain: in sunlit hours
    I loved that far-off hill of ours . . . .
The corn! So breathless was I for the flowers! –
    When these we'd gather up and bring,
      I'd sing.

5   I loved to pick . . . all that was small! . . .
          The grass; the cornflowers, I recall.
     The violet's scent I found – and, best of all,
           That of the cowslip at our feet –
               So sweet!

6   The daisies, too, whose pools of white
          Made Sunday walks a great delight:
    And birds on branches, singing! And the height –
           The firmament that shone on you –
               Was blue.

7   And Christmas Eve – the night one lays
          One's shoe beside the fire-place;
    I know I couldn't wait to wake, and race
           To sing the song I loved so well –
               'Noël'!

8   I loved Mama – her smile. Serene,
          It spoke of things that were not seen –
    'My joy is in Eternity! I mean
           To go and see the God of Love
               Above.

9   'And there my angels will receive
          Me . . . with the Virgin, I believe!
    To Jesus I will offer those I leave –
           Their heaviness, when weeping starts;
              Their hearts . . .'

10   And this I loved: the Host of white
            Came in the morning, to unite
My soul and His, paid court! And, with delight,
            I opened – flung its doors apart! –
                My heart.   ★[1]

11   My father, in the belvedere,
            Would kiss his child: how very dear
The light that came from him! I'd go up near
            To smoothe his head. His hair was so
                Like snow . . .

12   Thérèse and I, upon his knees,
            When evening came, would take our ease:
My cradle-days, you'd think, would never cease.
            And still his singing-voice, so clear
                I hear.

13   Reposeful memory! that brings
            The vivid sight of many things:
Our suppers . . . how the scent of roses clings! . . .
            Shrubs, blossoming, in Summer light
                Were bright.

14   In quiet, as the light grew less
            I would be merging with Thérèse! –
My soul and hers would, almost, coalesce . . .
            It was as though one heart would do
                For two.

15   And then our hands entwined, and we
                Sang, both, one Sacred Melody:
        A bride in Heav'n we each of us would be! –
            This, even then, did Carmel seem . . .
                Our dream.

16   Then: Italy and Switzerland –
                Skies blue . . . ripe fruit on every hand!
       But, best, to see the Holy Father stand
            And look – the Pontiff-Monarch: he
                At me.

17   Love made me kiss it, when I found
                The Colosseum's holy ground! –
       I heard how catacomb and vault resound.
            All answered, as I went along,
                My song . . .

18   Joys had to end, and tears to flow,
                Alarm had seized my spirit so.
       I donned my Spouse's arms for battle, though! –
            My good, His Cross . . . *that only* brought
                Support.   ★[2]

19   I loved – from worldly tumult free –
                To hear the echo, far from me.
     Tears came; I picked the flowers, could hardly see
        (The valley shaded, blossom-strown) –
                Alone.

20   I loved to hear the far-off bell
        (Its chime unclear) the Hours tell.
I'd sit down in the fields when evening fell
      And hear the breezes, going by . . .
          They'd sigh.

21   I loved to watch the swallows dart;
        The turtledoves, that coo, apart;
And insect wings . . . I heard them stop and start –
      Loved, as a murmured undertone
          Their drone.

22   I loved the pearl upon the lawn,
        Upon the Bengal roses borne: ★³
And – making honey since the crack of dawn! –
      So marvellous, the virgin bee
          To me!

23   I loved to pick the heather, turn
        And run upon the moss! I'd learn
To catch, as it vibrated on the fern,
      The butterfly, its wings shot-through
          With blue.

24   I loved the dusk; the worms that glowed:
        The night, where countless stars were sowed;
The moon! as on the sombre sky it rode,
      A disc of silver: at its height
          So bright!

25   I cared, in my young tenderness,
            For Father, aged now . . . ah, yes,
     He was my child, my riches – happiness!
            How tenderly I gave him this –
                My kiss!

26   The gentle lap of wave on stone
            We loved; the growling thunder-groan:
    Deep silence . . . then, the nightingale, alone –
            Out of the woods, and rising clear –
                We'd hear.

27   One day, the Crucifix he cast
            His gaze on, and he held it fast!
    Then looked at me . . . a pledge of love, his last:
            He gave it as for me alone –
                'My own.'

28   Then Jesus – for His hand was near –
            Took him who had been Céline's dear
   And bore him far above the hill that's here,
            To live beside Eternal Love,
                Above.

29   Now I, who fled the groves, belong
            Here – in Love's Prison (and it's strong!).
    I saw that things on earth do not last long.
            My joy in them would not abide:
                It died.

30   All crushed, the grass on which I'd stand,
                      The flower has withered in my hand . . .
          I'll run – I beg! – upon Your meadow-land;
                      My steps won't mark it as they fall
                            At all.

31   Now – as the stag, in burning heat,
                      Sighs for the water, flowing sweet,
         Jesus! I run to You, on falt'ring feet:
                      I need Your tears – a desert pool,
                            To cool.

32   Love draws me on, and they remain
                      Behind, my flock upon the plain.
        Bestir myself to guard them? I refrain! . . .
                      I only want to please the new
                            Lamb, You.

33   You, Jesus, are the Lamb I love
                    (And on that best one *can't* improve!);
        In You, I've all: the earth, and Heav'n above!
                    The Flower I pick, my King, is . . . who
                            But You!

34   *You*, Lily of the Valley! By
                      Your perfume I am charmed. I cry:
        'Bouquet of myrrh, O wreath of petals, I
                      Would love and keep You – on my heart,
                            Apart.'

35
    Your love is always here! In You,
     I've, still, the countryside I knew –
Woods, reeds . . . the far-off mountain, too:
     The rain . . . the sky with flakes of snow
       That blow.

36
    Yes, everything! the grain that grows;
     Half-opened flowers – I've all of those:
Forget-me-not, and buttercup, and rose,
     The lily-spray, by breezes bent –
       All scent!

37
    I've Solitude, whose strings can tell
     How cadences in Quiet dwell.
I've waterfalls, and rivers – rocks as well:
     The brook, its gentle murmurs heard;   ★[4]
       The bird.

38
    The rainbow; clarity at dawn;   ★[5]
     Our eyes to vast horizons drawn:
Greenery; foreign islands . . . and ripe corn;
     Butterflies: all the joy Spring yields
       In fields.

39
    Still – in Your love – I'm seeing, clear
     The palms, whose tops as gold appear
As much at night as when the dawn is here;
     What I have now will never cease –   ★[6]
       His Peace!

40   I've grapes I see and taste, anew;
            The dragonfly – delight to view!
     Strange-flowering virgin forest. Children, too,
           That sing; their heads hair-aureoled
               With gold.

41   In You, the springs, the hills, are mine:
            The water-lilies: still, entwine
    The honeysuckle . . . hawthorn, eglantine;
           And periwinkles! Poplars high
               Still sigh . . . .

42   And wind-crazed oats, that shake and cower;
           The gale, that's grave and full of power;
   Gossamer; fire ablaze; the shrubs in flower:
           The breeze, so gentle from the west;
               The nest.

43   In You, the lake; the silent wood
           Which right across the valley stood;
  The wave that spreads, on sand, its silver flood;
        Pearls, coral; treasures manifold   ★[7]
             Seas hold.

44   The vessel leaving harbour for
           The path of golden tide; the shore:
  Festoons of red the clouds above us wore
           The hour the downward sun retires:
             Its fires.

45   The dove, of softest purity . . . .
      Under my habit, giv'n to me,
   In You, I've necklace, gems, and finery.
      I've rings and diamonds – all are mine:
        They shine!

46   The shining star: Love doesn't fail
      To give its tokens often – they'll
   Disclose themselves! I see, as through a veil,
      When dusk is spreading on our land,
        Your hand.

47   You all the worlds there *are* sustain,
      Deep forests for the earth ordain
   (You blink Your eye, and they spring up again!) –
      It's following my every move,
        Your Love!

48   And I've your Heart, your Face – You show
      The arrow-shaft that wounds me so; ★[8]
   And, Lord, Your sacred lips that kiss me. Oh,
      Jesus, I love You. I'll pursue
        But You.

49   I'll sing the praise of sacred love
      Among the angels' ranks, above!
   And soon, I beg you, Jesus, may it prove –
      Oh, let me die of love, one day,
        I pray.

50   Flame-drawn, the wingèd insect (see!) ★[9]
           Will hurtle to the fire . . . To be
    The same – Your Love, my Hope, is drawing me –
          I'll fly to it, and in my turn
             Will burn!

51   I hear, O God . . . yes, even now –
          Your Heav'nly Feast is ready! How
  (My harp hung mute upon the willow-bough)
        I'll rush – Your knees I'll scramble to! –
             To You.

52   And I'll see Mary, near You – share
         As family, the Saints. That's where
  I'll find again – my exile over, there! –
        My Home, within the Father's Love
            Above!

Notes

PN 18

28 April 1895

'It now remains for me to speak of my dear Céline, the little companion of my childhood . . .' (*Aut.*, Ms. A).

Though this poem draws on Céline's thoughts and is written as though the 'I' were Céline, it echoes with memories of Thérèse's own life: her early childhood, the Sunday walks in Alençon 'when Mama used to accompany us'; Les Buissonnets in Lisieux, where 'my life was truly happy'; the 'shoe beside the fireplace' on Christmas Eve (occasion of the significant 'grace of conversion' after Midnight Mass) – though *this* shoe is Céline's, at Alençon;

the trip to Switzerland and Italy in 1887: and Céline and she – confidantes of each other's thoughts – seeing in the belvedere the 'white moon rising gently over the tall trees'.

Two years after this, Thérèse sent ten of the stanzas (with slight variations of wording) to the Abbé Bellière, under the title *Whoever has Jesus, has all.*

St. 5, l. 1 'all that was small': Thérèse uses the diminutives 'herbettes' and 'fleurettes' for grass and flowers, going on to specify 'cornflowers'.

St. 9, l. 1 'my angels': the four children who had died in infancy.

St. 10, l. 2 'in the morning': Fr., 'the morning of my life'. The stanza refers to First Communion.

'to unite': see Thérèse's description of her own First Communion in *Aut.* (Ms. A).

St. 13, l. 4 'Shrubs': in the French, *Les Buissonnets*, 'the little bushes'; the name of their family home.

Sts. 16–17 The pilgrimage Louis made, with Céline and Thérèse, in 1887.

St. 21 This stanza was omitted in 1898, but reinstated in subsequent editions.

St. 27, l. 5 'My own': *'Ma part'* (my portion) was in inverted commas as written by Thérèse and perhaps refers to a phrase in the Psalms.

St. 33, l. 2 Lit., 'You are enough for me, O supreme Good!'

St. 33, ll. 4–5 Thérèse quotes words written by Céline herself in an unsuccessful attempt at a poem.

St. 41, l. 1 'springs', i.e. of water.

St. 47, ll. 4–5 The French (manuscript, and later editions of *Histoire d'une Ame*) speaks of God's constant 'gaze of love'.

★[1] P here omits a stanza referring to Céline's seeking the Creator in nature.

★[2] P here omits a stanza about Céline deprived of her family; and another stanza recounting a dream of Céline's.

★[3] 'Bengal roses' is P's.

★[4] As Th constructed the poem, this line and the next are at the end of St. 39, above numbering. (Th, in St. 37, specifies a number of animals of the countryside). In an earlier and superseded draft Th herself placed the present two lines where they are here; P followed this.

★[5] 'clarity at dawn' (lit. 'the pure dawn') is P's.

★[6] See note ★[4]. The lines with which P concluded stanza 39 are Th's own (only the tense different), taken from a stanza which P had deleted earlier, see ★[1]. P's thoughtful change to stanza 39 may be said to improve it.

★[7] P specifies coral among Th's varied treasures of the sea.

★[8] 'arrow-shaft' is P's, but is implied in Th's reference to wounding. Th wrote of God's 'sweet gaze'; this is what the line refers to.

★[9] The reference to an 'insect' (Th wrote 'butterfly') is P's. This perhaps did *not* improve the poetry.

19

HYMN TO THE HOLY FACE

1   Your picture, Jesus, like a star
     Is guiding me! Ah, well You know
     Your Features – grace itself they are –
     To me, are Heaven here below.
     Your weeping . . . that, to Love, appears
     As ornament – attractiveness!
     I'm smiling while *I'm* shedding tears
     At seeing You in your distress.

2   To comfort You, I want to be
     Unknown, in loneliness. Below   ★
     Your Beauty's veiled, and yet to me
     Reveals its Mystery! and, oh,
     Would I, to You, were flying free!

3   Your Face . . . my only Homeland, and
     The Kingdom, too, where Love has sway:
     And it's my smiling meadowland,
     The gentle Sun of every day:
     The Lily of the Valley – ah,
     Its perfume's Mystery! I'm giv'n
     What consolation from afar! –
     A foretaste of the Peace of Heav'n.

4   Your Face, that has such tenderness
     Is like a sweet reposeful lyre . . .
     Bouquet of Myrrh, I would caress
     (Such gentleness do You inspire!),
     That safely to my heart I'd press . . . .

5   Your Face . . . ah, only that will be
           The wealth I ask as revenue:
           I'll hide in it, unceasingly;
           Then, Jesus, I'll resemble You!
           Imprint in me those traits divine
           Your Gentleness of Face imparts;
           Holiness, then, will soon be mine –
           To You I'll be attracting hearts!

6   So I can gather souls – it's this,
           A golden harvest, I desire –
           Consume me; give me soon, in bliss,
           That tender burning of Your Fire,
           Your lips in an eternal Kiss!

Notes

PN 20

12 August 1895

'*O dear Face of Jesus!* in awaiting the eternal day when we shall contemplate your infinite Glory, our only desire is to charm your *Divine Eyes* in hiding our features too, so that here below no one would be able to recognize us ... your *Veiled Gaze*, that is our *Heaven, O Jesus!* ' (Conclusion of Thérèse's Act of Consecration to the Holy Face, August 1896.)

The picture mentioned is one of the Veil of Veronica, on which, according to tradition, the thorn-crowned face of Christ was imprinted at the time of the Passion. 'She (Thérèse) had a great devotion to the Holy Face of Jesus, and she spoke to me constantly of her desire to resemble him': Sr Marie of the Trinity to the diocesan tribunal.

★ 'in loneliness', lit. 'solitary.' P added this to Th's reference to her, Thérèse's, wish to be 'unknown' – as she was in Carmel (but not after her death).

20

YOU HAVE BROKEN
MY BONDS, O LORD!

*Written to celebrate the entry into Carmel
of her cousin, Marie Guérin.*

1   O Jesus! it's today ' you break my bonds, and I
Know why this Order here ' the Virgin Mary's – drew
Me to this quiet place: ' I'll find *true good*; that's why
I've left (though they're so dear) ' my family, for You:
Celestial favours, though, ' their recompense will be.
And sinners pardoned! – *that* ' is what You'll give to me . . .

2   Carmel's my chosen home, for so
Oases draw! Your Love
                now calls me! I declare:
    It's there, it's there, that I want to go,
    To love and soon, then, to die.   ★
    It's there I'd follow You – oh,
    It's there, it is there!

3   O Jesus, it's today ' You make my waiting cease!
Now I can be before ' the Eucharist engrossed,
Can immolate myself, ' awaiting Heaven's peace;
And, open to the Sun, ' the heart-rays of the Host,
In loving You as though ' a Seraph, I will stay:
Lord, in this hearth of Love ' I now will burn away.

4   Soon, Jesus, I must follow, to
          Eternal shores, from earth:
                      to me may it be giv'n
          Always, always, in Heaven, with You,
          To love, no longer to die . . . . :
          Always, in Heaven with You –
          In Heav'n! yes, in Heav'n! . . .

Notes

PN 21

15 August 1895, Feast of the Assumption

'It's in your footsteps . . . that I would like to see my little Marie walking. You will be her model! Poor child! how hard these last days are for her! . . . It seems to me that the time [Marie Guérin's entry into Carmel] will never come, yet it is approaching with great strides. I ask the good God that she may be a holy religious like you, Thérèse.' (Letter to Thérèse from her aunt, Céline Guérin, 28 July 1895.)

St. 3, l. 1 'make my waiting cease': lit., 'fulfil all my desires' (*combles tous mes voeux*).

★ 'soon': P added this.

TO THE SACRED HEART

1 Seeking her Jesus, to the Sepulchre,
   Weighed down and crying, Mary Magdalene
   Came, and the angels wished to comfort her,
   But nothing could assuage her sorrow then.
   Archangels in your splendour! it was not
   You who could satisfy her soul that day.
   To cradle there the Angels' Lord – that's what
   She'd come to do: to take Him far away . . . .

2 She came before the day had broken . . . (who
   Had been the last to leave the tomb? This one):
   Though hidden still His light, her God *came too* –
   By Mary's love He would not be outdone!
   Disclosing first His Blessed Face, one word
   He spoke – His heart a torrent in release!
   For Jesus murmured 'Mary', and she heard
   What gave her back her happiness and peace.

3 Once, Madeleine's was also *my* desire:
   To see You and approach You, God, I'd fling
   My heart-gaze into endless air, aspire
   To seeking there its Master and its King.
   Seeing the flowers and birds, the starry blue,
   The lucid waters, brilliant though they be,
   I'd cry: 'If I don't see my God, then you,
   Nature, are just a mighty tomb for me!

4   'My need: a heart that burns with tenderness;
     Where – ever a support – my head can lay;
     That, loving me – my frailty no less,
     The whole of me! – won't leave me, night or day!'
     But no created being could I find
     Who here on earth would love me deathlessly.
     I must have *God* to put on humankind –
     Become my Brother, suffering for me.

5   You heard me, Spouse I love! You wished to be
     My heart's delight, and came . . . to *die*: Your will
     The shedding of Your blood – what mystery! . . .
     You're living for me, on the altar still.
     I cannot see the glory of Your Face,
     Or hear Your voice's tones – how gentle, those:
     I *can*, O God, live wholly by Your grace.
     Upon Your Sacred Heart is my repose!

6   Dear Heart of Jesus! tender Treasure, You
     In whom, alone, my joy and hopes reside:
     You charmed me in my youth that's tender too –
     Stay! up to my last evening by my side.
     O Heart of Jesus, giv'n to You alone,
     My life belongs to Goodness Infinite . . . .
     You know – all my desires to You are known –
     I want my being to be lost in It!

7   I know, in all our acts of justice, we
     Have nothing that's of value to You: so
     My sacrifices . . . all, as in a sea –
     To give them worth – into Your Heart I throw.
     You found the Angels flawed when they were tried:
     In light'ning Your Commandments were conveyed.
     O Jesus, in Your Sacred Heart I hide:
     My virtue . . . it is You. I'm not afraid.

8   I know one must – to have the power to see
            Your Glory – first a path of fire have trod:
            My Purgatory I would like to be
            Your burning Flame of Love, O Heart of God!
            My exile over, I would like to make
            An act of love – pure love – as I depart;
            And, flying to my Homeland then, to take
            A place – directly – in Your Sacred Heart!

Notes

PN 23

21 June or October 1895

Céline relates how Thérèse spoke to her about a kaleidoscope they had played with when young: '. . . pretty patterns of different colours; if one turns the instrument it produces infinite variations.' Thérèse takes the kaleidoscope to pieces and discovers only 'some little bits of paper and cloth thrown here and there', and three mirrors. For her this was 'the image of a great mystery. So long as our actions, no matter how small, remain within the focus of love, the Blessed Trinity . . . gives them an admirable reflection and beauty . . .' (*Conseils et Souvenirs*).

This poem, like Poems 5 and 32, was written for Sr Marie of the Sacred Heart. On 9th June Thérèse had made her Act of Offering to Merciful Love.

St. 3, l. 3 'endless air': lit., 'immense plain' (*l'immense plaine*). I have taken
    this to refer to the skies, as in line 5, and Poem 39, St. 4 (*la plaine azurée*).
St. 4, l. 7 Thérèse wrote of God being *able* to suffer, having taken human
nature at the Incarnation.

22

JESUS, MY LOVE, RECALL!

1   Recall how from Your Father's glory You –
From heav'nly splendours, from Your Home above –
Came down to us: what did You come to do?
To buy all sinners back, because of love.
A mite, in Mary's womb
                as though to an abyss
You came, Your grandeur veiled . . .
                    Infinite glory – this?
          A Second Heaven's rest
          You found: on Mary's breast –
             Ah, this recall!

2   And now recall: at Your Nativity
The Angels, too, came down! Their praises rang:
'To God, all Glory, Power and Honour be,
And peace on earth to friends of God,' they sang.
For nineteen-hundred years
                You've kept Your promise, Lord:
How rich Your children! – peace
               into their souls is poured.
        I come – because Your peace,
        Prodigious, will not cease! –
          To You, my All.

3   I come; so wrap me in Your swaddling-clothes –
For ever hidden in Your crib I'd stay! –
Recalling, as angelic music flows,
The laughter then of ev'ry joyous day.

The Shepherds and the Kings
                    remember, Jesus, too:
In joy, they offered hearts
                    in fealty to You.
          The Innocents – outpoured
          Their life-blood for You, Lord –
                    All these recall.

4   Recall that Mary's arms, to You her Son
         Were more appealing than Your royal throne!
         And You, to stay alive, O little one,
         Relied upon the Virgin's milk alone:
Oh, what a feast of love
                    Your Mother gives to You,
My little Brother – may
                    I, Jesus, be there too!
          Your Mother – Sister – sweet
          Gave You Your own heart-beat:
                    This, too, recall.

5   And Joseph, then – the humble man You would
         Call 'Father' – snatched and took, by Heav'n's command
         You (sleeping on Your Mother's breast . . . Your blood
         Sought furiously!) to a foreign land . . . .
You, Word of God, and yet –
                    what Mystery! – so meek
That You kept silence – You –
                    and made an angel speak!
          That far-away exile
          Beside the River Nile
                    Oh, that recall.

6   Your Mother holds You, under different skies
     (I picture them at night, as cloudless blue):
     The stars of gold attract Your baby eyes;
     The moon, of silver, is enchanting You.
  That hand, caressing hers
         gave life to humankind
  As You upheld the world
       by keeping it in mind!
     Of *me* (my soul can sing)
     You thought, my little King –
       Oh, that recall.

7   Recall this too: that when You were alone
     You worked (the hands of *God* worked hard!); You'd show
     You sought to be forgotten and unknown –
     Rejecting human ways in doing so.
  Although to charm the world
        one word of Yours would do,
  It pleased you more to hide
       the Wisdom that is You . . .
     Appearing not to know! –
     You, Lord, Almighty! . . . oh,
       All that recall.

8   Recall: You were a nomad! – You would roam,
     A stranger on the earth, Eternal Word!
     You'd nothing; not a stone was Yours, no home:
     You – shelterless as if You were a bird.
  Live, Jesus, now in *me*;
        come, lay Your head and rest –
  My soul is ready now
       for You to be its Guest:

My Love, my Saviour, come,
It's Yours, this heart, the Home
Of You my All.

9   Recall those signs of special tenderness
      You showered on the smallest ones: I, too,
      Would like to be receiving Your caress,
      Your kisses: these delights I ask of You.
    To come to You, in Heav'n
                    where joy is shining clear,
    The virtues of a child
                    I'll know to practise here;
            Your Heaven, the reward
            Of 'little children', Lord –
              This, now recall.

10   Recall the one who, at the well, believed
      The Stranger coming weary from the road:
      The woman of Samaria received
      That love with which Your breast had overflowed.
    Ah, yes, I know the One
                    who asked a drink of me:
    He is the Gift of God
                    the fount of glory: He
            Is Water that will flow
            And give me Life! I know –
              I hear Your call . . .

11   You call: 'Poor souls, so laden, come to Me;
      Your burdens will be lightened soon! And learn –
      You, plunged for ever in my Heart, will be
      Clear founts of Life to others, in your turn.'
    I'm thirsty, Jesus, for
                    this Water! Like a sea,

Let torrents, O my God,
            flood in and cover me –
Love's Ocean my abode!
I come – without my load,
            To You, my All!

12   Recall the sorry tale: this child of light
        Often, alas, neglects the King Above.   ★¹
        Oh, pity her in this her wretched plight,
        Grant pardon, Jesus, from Your Heart of Love!
Oh, give me grace and skill
            to know of ways divine:
And from the Gospel's words
            may hidden secrets shine.
        Such treasure does it hold,
        I find it purest gold:
            Oh, that recall.

13   Recall that she who bore and mothered You
        Has sway upon Your Heart! Of this, a sign
        Is that You once, when she had asked You to,
        Changed water into most delicious wine.
I beg – transform *my* works;
            let imperfection be
Perfection by Your power
            enacted at her plea.
        That I'm her child . . . oh, may
        You often, Lord, I pray,
            This now recall.

14   Recall, as well, that often You would seek
        The hills at evening, when the sun was low.
        Recall the words of love Your Heart would speak –
        Your prayer, with all the world asleep below.

Your orisons, O God,
                    I offer with delight:
My prayers, my Office – *all*
                    with them I can unite!
            There, near Your Heart, I sing
            My joyous offering!
                    Ah, that recall.

15   And, seeing golden wheat . . . as though You'd count
            The harvest-ears with which a field was decked,
            You saw the sheaves upon Your holy mount,
            You murmured then the names of the elect.
        To help Your Harvest soon
                        be gathered, every day
        I sacrifice myself:
                        to You, O God! I pray
                The harvesters will gain
                From all my joy and pain:
                        I beg, recall!

16   Recall: how all the angels celebrate
            (Their singing fills the vaults of Heav'n anew –
            What joy they have!) when they can contemplate
            One sinner who lifts up his eyes to You.
        And I . . . I'd like to add
                        to their high jubilee:
        O Jesus, I will pray
                        for sinners, ceaselessly!
                I came to Carmel – why?
                To people Heaven, I
                    Can say! . . . Recall.

17   Recall, my God: that that exquisite Flame
    You willed to light in hearts has sought me out!
    That Blaze from Heav'n! – into my soul it came;
    I want to spread its burnings all about.
For, just a feeble spark –
        no more does one require
(O mystery of life!)
        to light a forest fire:
    For this my strivings are –
    To make it travel far!
      Oh, that recall.

18   Recall . . . ah, what a feast that one would be
    Which welcomed back, as son, the penitent!
    Recall: the soul which has simplicity
    Gets – every moment – *You* as Nourishment . . . .
O Jesus, your Heart-beats
       a prodigal can know
(Those floods of love for *me*
       are boundless, also, though):
    My love! my King Divine,
    Your fortune now is mine,
      Jesus, recall.

19   Recall Your scorn of earthly glory; when
    You showered on us miracles, You cried:
    'O you, who seek the vain esteem of men,
    How can you be believers, in your pride? –
My works amaze you now,
       but soon will come the hour
When friends of mine, yet more,
       work wonders by my power.'

My Spouse, my Jesus, You
Were humble, meek (I, too
Must be). Recall.

20   Recall: as though inebriate, St John,
        Apostle-Virgin, rested on Your breast.
        Pure tenderness was what he lay upon:
        He knew Your Secrets in that holy rest!
    That Loved Disciple can
                    no jealousy arouse –
    I know Your Secrets, too,
                    O Lord! I am Your spouse.
        My Saviour, I'm caressed,
        I'm lulled, upon the breast
            Of You, my All.

21   Your Agony recall . . . enduring it,
        You wept; a sweat of blood began to flow:
        Those pearls of love – their worth is infinite! –   ★[2]
        Have made a crop of virgin flowers grow.
    An angel showing then
                    this harvest, You foresaw
    What brought Your soul again
                    the joy it had before.
        And that You saw *me* so,
        Among Your lilies – oh,
            Jesus, recall!

22   Your blood, Your tears – so fruitful were they – made,
        Here blossoming, these virgin flowers of earth
        Be able to be mothers also: they'd
        Present You many hearts they bring to birth.
    I'm virgin, Jesus: I –
                    mysterious, though true –

Do this! I mother souls
                    in being one with You.
              In saving sinners, ours
              Such joy! All virgin flowers,
                    I beg, recall.

23   Recall – in sweat and blood and suffering
          A Man condemned to death lifts up His eyes,
          And: 'In my power, and *soon*,' declares this King,
          'You'll see me, glorious in Paradise!'
This man, the Son of God! –
                    but who believed it? Men
Did not desire to, with
                    His glory hidden then.
              The Prince of Peace, who dies! . . .
              I look, and recognize
                    You are my All.

24   Recall: Your Face – the Face of God – would be
          Unrecognized by those who were Your own!
          You've left Your lovely portrait, though, for me:
          I recognize You. You are not unknown.
I recognize You – yes,
                    Eternal One! Your Face
Seen even through your tears
                    has won me by its grace . . . .
              Your tears (as in a cup)
              Souls, loving, gather up –
                    Jesus, recall!

25   Recall that plaint – of love for us, that came
          From You upon the Cross: for, out it burst,
          It flooded from Your Heart. In me, the same
          Imprints itself! I share that burning thirst.

The more I feel Your Flame,
　　　　　　　　the more I've got to do
To slake the burning. How?
　　　　　　　　In giving souls to You!
　　　　　That thirst of love, I say,
　　　　　Burns in me, night and day –
　　　　　　Oh, that recall.

26　　　　Recall, O Jesus, Word of Life, to show
　　　　　Your love, You died for me! and so I, too
　　　　　Wish in return to love *You*, madly – oh!
　　　　　I, also, wish to live and die for You.
　　　You know it, O my God!
　　　　　　　　　my one desire's to make
　　　You loved, and then to be
　　　　　　　　　a martyr for Your sake!
　　　　　Of love I wish to die:
　　　　　Lord, that I want this, I
　　　　　　Beg You recall.

27　　　　Recall this, too: 'How happy, anyone' –
　　　　　You said to us, Your Victory achieved –
　　　　　'Who, though he has not yet beheld the Son
　　　　　As gloriously risen, has believed.'
　　　In peace – adoring You
　　　　　　　　　in dark but loving state,
　　　I'll see You when it's dawn,
　　　　　　　　O Jesus! – I will wait.
　　　　　My wish, my Lord so dear,
　　　　　Is not to see You *here* –
　　　　　　Oh, that recall!

28   You couldn't leave us orphans, though You were
          Ascending to the Father.   In disguise,
          You stayed and made Yourself our Prisoner! –
          You veiled Your risen glory from our eyes.
Yet though Your veil is dark,
                    it's pure and luminous:
Faith says: 'The Bread of Heav'n
                    is nourishment for us':
          Love's mystery! – I'm fed
          Each day by Living Bread –
          Jesus . . . my All.

29   Though, Sacrament of Love, You have Your foes . . .
          In spite of all the blasphemies You face . . .
          You show how much You love me – for You chose
          To come and make my heart Your dwelling-place!
Divine and holy Host!
                    Yourself as Bread You give:
I live – no longer I,
                  it's by Your Life I live.
          Ciborium of gold
          Most dear to You, *I* hold
          Jesus, my All!

30   Jesus, my All – oh, may my heart remain
          Your sanctuary: stay here, Holy One! –
          This heart that wicked men cannot profane,
          A border where the flowers turn to the Sun.
White Lily – like the Sun!
                    if You should go away,
Then all my blossoms here
                  would wither in a day.

Jesus, my Lily-Flower,
Have, always, as Your bower
This heart, my All!

31   My wish is to console You in Your pain
At sinners who forget You, as they do.
My only Love! oh, grant me this as gain –
To have a thousand hearts for loving You!
Too few! Let Beauty then
        this greater grace impart:
Give me, to love You with,
        the Heart of God – Your Heart!
This, my desire (for I'm
Afire, and all the time!)
O Lord, recall.

32   Recall: in only this Your holy will
I find that heart's-repose by which I'm blest –
Submissive like a child, untroubled, still;
My Saviour, drowsing in Your arms, at rest!
Should *You* be drowsing too,
        though storms may rage around,
I'd stay for ever thus,
        the peace is so profound!
But, as You sleep, prepare
The waking up from there,
Jesus, my All!

33   Recall: the time for which I often sigh
Is when in clouds of glory You'll descend.
Oh, may your Angel come, at last, and cry:
'It's Judgment Day, and Time is at an end!'
And then, with what a rush
        I'll hurtle over space,

For, very near to You
                    I'll go and take my place!
        That You my Heav'n must be:
        My Home, eternally —
                    Oh, that recall!

Notes

PN 24

21 October 1895

Céline tells how she asked Thérèse to write a poem detailing (as Céline later says, self-deprecatingly) the 'immense sacrifices' she, Céline, had made for Jesus. Thérèse responded with this poem detailing (as Céline put it) the immense 'sacrifices of Jesus for me.'

St. 27, l. 5 Lit., 'In the darkness of Faith I love and adore You'
★¹ 'alas, neglects' is P's. Th's wording indicated that she often 'forgets' to be a good subject and servant-maid of the King.
★² 'pearls' is P's poetic word for dew.

23

MY LONGINGS BEFORE
THE TABERNACLE

1   O happy key, since you exist
    For this! – you open, every day,
    The prison of the Eucharist
    Where God, who's Love, is locked away!
    But I can turn the mortice (for
    My faith can do this wondrous thing) –
    Can open up the golden door,
    To hide, beside my Heav'nly King.

2   I'd like to burn away, to be
    Consumed – near God by day and night;
    A steady glow of mystery,
    A sanctuary lamp, alight.
    What happiness is mine: I've flame
    Within me! . . . Daily thus can I
    Win Jesus *souls*, and by the same
    Heart's-fire He came to light them by.

3   O Holy Altar-stone, you fill
    Me, every dawn, with envy too,
    As the Eternal, by His Will –
    A Bethlehem – is born on You.
    Then, enter in this soul (my Own,
    My Saviour!), since for You it burns:
    Far from the coldness of a stone,
    It's *that* for which Your own Heart yearns.

4 O Altar-cloth! where angels go –
   How, too, I envy you in this:
   I see my Jesus . . . there, as though
   In swaddling-clothes, my Treasure is!
   Change my heart, Mary! so I am
   An Altar-cloth that's pure and bright,
   Then may my heart receive your Lamb
   Who hides Himself . . . the Host of white.

5 Paten, I envy you as well! –
   Upon you Jesus takes His rest:
   May Endless Grandeur come and dwell
   (Though poor the lodging) as my Guest! . . .
   He's here with me – He doesn't wait
   Until the dusk of life I see:
   He comes, and – how my joy is great! –
   A living Monstrance makes of me.

6 Would I were you, to have your prize –
   The Blood of God, O happy Cup!
   But I, too, at the Sacrifice,
   Those precious drops can gather up.
   Much dearer Jesus values me
   Than golden Vases, jewel-set:
   The Altar a new Calvary,
   His Blood for me is flowing yet.

7 I am (O Jesus, Holy Vine,
   To whom all fruitfulness is due)
   A bunch of grapes – O King Divine! –
   That ought to disappear for You.
   It's in the Winepress – Suffering –
   That I'll be proving what I say:
   The joy of love to which I cling
   Is self-oblation, every day!

8   O happy lot! For, chosen there
           Among the grains of purest Wheat,
           I now may in their dying share,
           For Jesus: thus my joy's complete!
           I am Your spouse: You'll always be
           My Love – come live in me! I say:
           O come . . . You have enraptured me –
           Transform me into You, I pray!

Notes

PN 25

Autumn? 1895

'By ever greater devotion to Jesus in the Eucharist Thérèse enters more fully into the way of spiritual childhood. That participation in the Eucharistic mystery brings her to the perfection of abandonment . . . In the measure in which the creature consents to "lose herself" in God, she is completely possessed by Him . . .' (Père Victor de la Vièrge, *op. cit.*).

Thérèse wrote this poem at the request of Sr Saint Vincent de Paul.

———————————

St. 1, l. 1 In the French the envied key is 'little'.
St. 1, l. 7 'golden' is not in the French: but Thérèse refers, of course, to the tabernacle.

24

THE DIVINE LITTLE
BEGGAR-BOY OF CHRISTMAS:
Extracts from a play

*This play – written by Thérèse in 1895 for performance by the nuns in
the Lisieux Carmel at Christmas – opens with the appearance of an
angel, carrying the baby Jesus in his arms in the Bethlehem stable. He
invites the nuns to come forward, one by one, to offer gifts to the Child.
He specifies what gifts Jesus would most like. They include the
following:*

A golden throne

Jesus (your Treasure and your own!) –
Hear what to Him is very dear:
He asks of you a *golden throne*;
He finds none in the stable here.
A sinner is like that, alas –
This stable! Jesus, looking, sees
Nothing to joy His heart. He has
No place where He can take His ease.
       Save – this your goal –
       The sinner . . . his soul,
Since Jesus sighs there for His due.
       Still more – behold:
       As His throne of gold?
The *pure heart* that He wants from you!

Some milk

This Holy One – Himself their food –
Before whom saints in Heaven bow,
A Child, in His necessitude,

Is asking your assistance now.
From Heaven's bliss He came! . . . I plead –
Since poverty is now so near:
Sister, a *drop of milk* to feed
Jesus, your little Brother here!
    His smiles impart
    This, deep to your heart:
'That's what I love – simplicity!'
    Noël! Noël!
    On the earth I dwell:
You are the milk of love for me!

Some little birds

Sister, I see you burn to know
What little Jesus wants . . . Then I'll
Disclose it straightaway, and so
I'll tell you how to make Him smile:
Go catch some *little birds*, to fly
About the stable. Doing this,
They'll represent the charm, on high,
Of children loving Him in Bliss.
    Birdsong they sing,
    And their chirruping
Will make His tiny features shine.
    For children pray:
    In Heaven, one day,
Through *these* He will your crown entwine!

A star

And sometimes when a cloud of grey
Darkens and covers up the sky,
Jesus is sad, at close of day
With nothing then to light Him by.
To joy Him, let them all combine,

Your virtues, like a star at night –
A *scintillating star*, to shine:
Yes, you be now a burning light!
　　　To Heaven, raise
　　　Up eyes, by its blaze
That sinners pierce the veil. For, ah!
　　　This Child that's born,
　　　The Planet of dawn,
Has chosen *you* to be His star!

A lyre

Listen, my little Sister, may
I tell you now the Child's desire:
To have your heart, and on it play
His melodies, as on a lyre!
Heaven is filled with harmony –
The incense of the Angels: still,　★
Like theirs, He wants your praise to be
Ascending here, from Carmel's hill.
　　　Your heart is where,
　　　O Sister . . . from *there*
He wants the melody to rise:
　　　Yes, night and day,
　　　Love-song . . . as to say
'Here burns my life as sacrifice!'
. . . . . .

A valley

As by a blaze of sun we see
Nature is all made lovely, and
Vermilion fire gilds fetchingly
The valley and the meadowland,
So Jesus, Heaven's Sun divine,
Gilds all that He approaches to!
The glories of His morning shine

Brighter than fires of sunrise do.
>See Him arise,
>This Sun, in the skies! –
He sheds upon your exile dim
>His warmest beam,
>With His gifts that stream:
A *smiling valley* be for Him! . . .

Some harvesters

Below – another country there! –
Despite the snow, and winter's cold,
Protected by the Child with care,
The crops are ripening, to gold.
One needs, alas, to gather in,
Harvesters who, with hearts that burn,
Love suffering! and – souls to win –
View sword and flame with unconcern.
>Noël! Noël!
>I know very well
In Carmel you will wish this, too:
>Your Saviour pleads,
>O Sister: He needs
Many apostles, born of you!

A bunch of grapes

Sister, I wish that I were giv'n
A *bunch of golden grapes*! for I
Could then refresh the King of Heav'n –
His little mouth is very dry!
How sweet a lot is yours: regard –
You are the bunch that's pointed to:
The Child will take and *press you hard* –
His dainty hand has chosen you.

Too small is He,
Tonight yet, to be
Eating the grapes themselves, and so
What would He choose?
Ah, to taste the juice
From this, *His* golden honey-glow!

A little host

The Holy Child does this for you:
That He may to your soul convey
His Life, as food! transforms – into
Himself – a little host, each day.
And (with a love that's greater still)
He wants to change *you also* – yes,
Into Himself! He longs to fill
Your heart – His joy, His happiness.
Noël! Noël!
I come here, to tell
You what will be for your delight
The Lamb came to
Be small, and to you!
Be, therefore, *His pure host of white*!

A smile

The world has failed to recognize
His charm (your Spouse who so endears!)
And now I see – His gentle eyes
Are glistening with little tears.
Yet, you can give Him comfort who
Dear Sister, holds His arms out. So,
To charm Him, this I ask from you –
Always be smiling, here below!
For, see – does not that gaze of His
Say: 'When you look at one of these

Here the metre
at the end of the
stanzas changes.

Your sisters, and you *smile* – that is
Enough to make my weeping cease!'

A flower
White snows upon the pastures reign
And cutting frost is all around:
By Winter, with its dismal train,
The flowers are withered on the ground.
Yet, see this *Meadow-Flower* appear,
Delighting you (this baby-King
Here blossoming) – from Homelands clear
Where reigning is Eternal Spring.
Be, then, a *little flower*, and hide! –
A flower that in the grasses blows:
To be beside your Spouse, beside
The King of Heav'n, the Christmas Rose.

Some bread
To God the Father, every day,
In prayer how often this is said –
O Author of all good, you pray,
'Give us this day our daily bread.'
God, here, our little Brother made –
He suffers now from hunger, too!
So, Sister, hear His cry for aid –
He asks *a little bread* from you.
The Holy Child, be very sure,
Wants nothing but your love. I say:
'Give food to Him – a soul that's pure,
The *bread* to feed Him, every day!'

A mirror

A mirror – what a plaything, that
For any child you want to please!
You then will find him smiling, at
The other child he thinks he sees.
Your soul's a crystal . . . come, and see
This stable, where the Word has smiled:
Here, imaged in you, may there be
His charm – the charm of God-made-child!
Ah! be, then, a reflection true,
A *mirror*, where your Spouse can trace
What He so wants: to look at *you*
And see the glory of His Face.

A palace

To house the nobles of the land
Are palaces, embellished fair;
Whilst hovels, on the other hand –
The wretched find their shelter there.
So, look at this poor stable; see
(His glory He has veiled, from love)
The Beggar-child of Christmas! He
Has left His palace up above.
You poverty (I know) embrace;
Your peace of heart is there. Ah, how
He wants your heart as dwelling-place –
A fitting *palace* for Him – now.

A crown of lilies

How sinners crown that lovely head! –
The cruel thorn around Him goes.
God's graces you should prize instead,
Of which the world no longer knows.
O you of virgin soul! may He

Forget His grief because of you:
Give Him – His *royal crown* shall be –
Pure souls of sister-virgins, too.
Come, right up to His throne, and there,
To give this Child such pleasure, braid
A beauteous crown for Him to wear:
A crown of *shining lilies* made!

Notes

RP 5 (extracts)

Christmas 1895

'See, then, all that Jesus asks from us, He has no need of our works, but only of our love, for the same God who declares that *He has no need to tell us if He is hungry* is not afraid to *beg* a little water from the Samaritan woman . . . it was the love of His poor creature that the creator of the Universe was asking for' (*Aut.*, Ms. B).

In performing this play or 'pious recreation', the nuns of the Lisieux Carmel were allocated their individual stanzas by lot. That headed *A bunch of grapes* fell to Thérèse's lot.

Stanza headed *Some milk*, *ll.* 1–2: lit., 'The One who feeds the elect with his Holy and Divine Essence'.
Stanza headed *Some little birds*, *ll.* 7–8: 'on high/in Bliss'. I have thought this to be implied; it is not explicit in the French.
Stanza headed *A little host*, *l.* 8: 'His joy, His happiness' refers to 'heart'. The French says 'treasure' also.
★ 'incense' (appropriate to Th's metaphor of burning, later in the stanza) is P's addition.

25

THE ANGEL OF THE DESERT

Extract from a play, *The Flight into Egypt*

1   I sing the Holy Family! they are
     The glory that is here attracting me:
     Here, in the desert . . . yet, this shining star
     Charms more than all the lights of Heav'n I see.
     Ah, who could look and understand this thing? –
     Among them, yet rejected by His own!
     See Jesus *moving on* – yes, wandering
     Upon the earth: His beauty all unknown.

2   But if the great are fearful of Your sway –   ★¹
     O King of Heaven, so-mysterious Light! –
     Long have You been desired by hearts today;
     In You the wretched find their Hope is bright.
     Abyss of Wisdom! Word, Who ever Is!   ★²
     Your gifts (that never can description fit)
     You give the small, the poor – so lavish, this!
     Their names in Heaven by Your Hand are writ.

3   Since in Your image ev'ry soul is made,
     The ignorant – if they are *humble*, too –
     Share in Your Wisdom! You, to sinners' aid
     Stoop down. You save them, calling them to You.
     The day will come when lamb and lion graze
     Untroubled in one pasturage, the same:
     The desert – *Your Land now*! – in other days
     Will more than once re-echo with Your Name.

4 For, by Your hearth of Love, O hidden God,
  Souls virginal will burn with zeal and thus ★³
  Will rush to where Your royal feet have trod,
  And deserts of the world be *populous*...
  Seraphic souls – hearts, blazing – will rejoice
  The angels who, like me, in Heaven dwell:
  Their hymns to God, though sung in homely voice,
  Will cause to quail the dark abyss of Hell.

5 Satan is base; in jealousy he would
  De-people deserts with a furious curse!
  Infinite Power he has not understood –
  A feeble *Child*... new to the universe!
  He has not understood the virgins who
  Have rest of spirit in their ardency.
  He has not understood their *power*, too,
  United to their Saviour, they and He.

6 Perhaps, O God, Your spouses, too, one day
  Will suffer Your own exile in their turn;
  The sinners, though, who'll send them all away
  Won't quench the flames of love with which they burn:
  And sacrilegious hate, a world impure,
  Can't dull such heav'nly whiteness or affect
  The virgins of the Lord (of that be sure):
  White vesture, and its snow will not be specked.

7 Ungrateful world, your reign is ending now:
  A little Child!... do you not see this sight –
  He gathers, joyfully, the martyr's-bough,
  The golden rose: the lily, brilliant white! ★⁴
  Do you not see His faithful virgins wait,
  Whose lamps of love shine out in one array?
  Do you not see? – that high Eternal Gate
  Will, for the holy, open up one day.

8   How happy the elect when they achieve
               Exchange for their *own* love! and they are giv'n
               Such beauty of appearance, and receive
               Eternity, for loving, up in Heav'n!
               No suffering! their exile ended – for
               They have attained to their repose above;
               Their exile ended – faith and hope no more –
               Peace only, and an ecstasy of love. ★⁵

Notes

RP 6 (extract)

21 January 1896, Feast of St Agnes

'. . . you explained to me the life of Carmel, which seemed to me very beautiful! . . . I felt that Carmel was the *desert* where the Good God was wanting me, also, to fly, to hide myself.' (*Aut.*, Ms. A)

★¹ 'are fearful of' (probably alluding to King Herod) is P's; Th had 'scorn'.
★² 'Word, Who ever Is' (*Verbe éternel*) is P's.
★³ 'zeal' is P's.
★⁴ 'golden rose' is P's. In the next line Th wrote of Jesus giving His own martyr's palm and lily to the faithful virgins.
★⁵ P substituted 'peace' for Th's 'joy', as in Poem 41.

[26]

HYMN OF SAINT AGNES

1   My Love is Christ: He is
                my very life, and He
    Is promised to me! None
                is to these eyes as dear:
    Already, of His sweet
                celestial harmony
      The melodies I hear.

2   He has adorned my hand,
                these matchless pearls are mine:
    My neck He beautified
                with strings of costly gem;
    These heav'nly rubies, too   ★[1]
                that now as ear-rings shine! –
      Oh, joy . . . He gave me them.

3   And jewels deck my hair –   ★[2]
                these He has given me;
    I wear already – look,
                it gleams! – His wedding ring:
    My virgin's mantle . . . pearls
                embroider it, to be
      One mass of glistering.

4   *I'm* promised, too! – to Him
                    the Angel Host obeys:
    Him they will never cease
                    to serve in awe, and that
    Is how the moon and sun,
                    in silence, tell His praise . . . .
      His Beauty wondered at.

5   Divine His Nature, Heav'n
                    His empire, and He chose
    His Mother here below,
                    a Virgin without spot.
    His Father is true God –
                    pure Spirit: never was
      A time when He was not.

6   In loving Christ (I touch
                    Him with my finger-tips),
    That loving makes me yet
                    more pure in spirit be:
    Virginity – as though
                    He's brushed me with His lips –
      Is treasure given me.

7   He has already put
                    His sign upon my face
    To make no lover dare
                    to pay me his address.
    My heart is – ah! sustained
                    by Him, He gives me grace,
      This King of kindliness.

8   His Blood has given me
                    such colour! and it is
     As if in the delights
                    of Heaven *now* I share –
     Already! This I can
                    take from His sacred kiss:
          There's milk and honey there.

9   And nothing do I fear –
                    not sword or flame! I'm free
     From all that could impair
                    my peace. I do not doubt
     That this great fire of love
                    that's now consuming me
          Will never be put out! . . .

Notes

PN 26

21 January 1896

'My Lord Jesus Christ hath betrothed me with his ring, and like a bride hath adorned me with a crown' (Antiphon, Office of St Agnes).

'To expect that God will "fill the hungry with good things" to the point of making them self-reliant and independent of Him would be a contradiction in terms. Always God's method of enriching us is to make us more dependent, more willing to find our completion in Him alone.' (Sr Teresa Margaret, D.C.)

★[1] 'rubies' is P's. Th wrote of ear-rings of diamond.
★[2] The image of jewels *in the hair* is P's, not Th's. Th wrote only of being adorned with precious stones.

[27]

SWEET REMEMBRANCE

A memento of the day of Céline's Profession

1
What could I ever compare
To this lovely day of days? –
Its sweetness utterly rare,
I shall cherish it, *always*.

2
I am bound to Jesus by
That binding which Love is owed,
Because Grandeur from on high
Has made me His own abode.

First refrain
My heart, intoxicated, turns
Into one love-pulsing thing! –
For now, in this body, burns
The Heart of my Spouse and King.

3
Now exile can bring no pain,
With Him – no wish to be free;
So soft are the bonds that chain
Ah, this *Jealous God* and me:

4
O You, Jealousy Divine –
A shaft through my heart it goes! –
For all my life You'll be mine,
My joy, and my sweet repose.

Second refrain
Jesus! consume this self, that so
You'll be, oh, my everything.
Henceforth I would be as though
A veil that will clothe my King.

Notes

PN 27

24 February 1896

'Memento of the most beautiful of days . . . the day containing and confirming all the graces Jesus and Mary showered upon their beloved Céline . . .' (Thérèse's inscription on holy picture).

───────────────

Second refrain 2, l. 2 Lit., 'Jesus alone must live in me.'

[28]

THE ETERNAL HYMN,
SUNG FROM EXILE

1   Your bride, who's exiled here
                 upon this foreign shore,
        Can yet sing hymns of love,
                 eternal her desire,
        For, O my Jesus! as
                 in Heav'n for evermore,
        So here on earth Your Love
                 enflames her with its Fire!

2   No greater Beauty can there be
        Than You – who give Yourself to me:
            But, in return,
            My Jesus . . . see! –
        My *life* one act of love, with which I burn.

3   You (heedless of its poverty,
               To live there!) to my heart repair:
               My feeble love – what mystery! –
               Suffices, Lord, to chain You there.

4   Oh Love – I'm ablaze –
               This soul be Your place! –
               Come here, of Your grace.
               Come here, *consume me.*

5 Your ardour's design
  Finds answer (it's mine):
  'The Furnace Divine
  My deeps ever be!'

6 Now, Lord, suffering
  Is pleasure! I sing:
  My love taking wing
  Towards You, I soar.

7 My Homeland alight
  My joy at its height,
  My soul, in delight
  With You, evermore!

8 My Homeland alight
  My joy at its height –
  You – *Love* – I live for!

Notes

PN 28

1 March 1896

Thérèse said that the Director of her soul, 'who is Jesus, does not teach me to count my acts; He educates me to do *everything* for love, to refuse Him nothing, to be pleased when He gives me an opportunity to prove to Him that I love Him . . .' (Thérèse, letter to Céline, 6 July 1893).

This poem was written for the feast-day of Sr Marie of St Joseph on 19 March.

On 21 March, Mère Marie de Gonzague would be re-elected Prioress. On the night of 2–3 April Thérèse's grave illness would declare itself in her first coughing of blood.

29

COMMENT ON THE DIVINE

*In adapting a published French translation
of the Spanish poem* Glosa a lo divino *by
St John of the Cross, Thérèse added touches
that were distinctively her own.*

Supported without any Support,
Without Light and in the Shadows,
I go, consumed by Love.

1   The world (to my great happiness)
Has had – for ever! – my farewells . . . .
Raised up, above myself, I've . . . yes,
God's my Support, and nothing else.
That which I value, I extol –
What being near to Him has taught
Is this: to see and feel my soul
Supported, but with no support!

2   I suffer, yes! from lack of Light
(One's life is short and fugitive):
At least, though, in this earthly night
In Love Celestial I live! . . . .
Though on this path which leads above
Unnumbered perils may appear,
My will is to endure, by Love,
The Shadows of my exile here.

3   I know this as reality:
The good, the bad in me – the whole,
Love's Power draws profit from, for He
Into *Himself* transforms my soul.
Fire burns inside my soul; it came
My heart – for always! – to endue.
I walk in Love's enchanting flame.
It always will consume me through.

Notes

PN 30

30 April 1896

Using an image employed by St John of the Cross, Thérèse, in her auto-biography, wrote of iron which desires 'to be identified with the fire in such a way that it is penetrated by, and absorbed in, its burning substance and seems to be but one with it . . . I ask Jesus to draw me into the flames of His love, to unite me so closely to Him that He lives and acts in me . . .' (Ms. C).

The French translation from which Thérèse made her poem is one by the Carmelites of Paris, published in 1877. Thérèse used many phrases from that version (even whole lines) but achieved a polish and a vivacity which the earlier version lacked. That version – like the Spanish of St John of the Cross – has stanzas of nine lines; Thérèse's stanzas have eight.

30

I THIRST FOR LOVE!
Written for Sister Marie of the Trinity
and of the Holy Face

1   You, Jesus – God – an exile here below,
Gave up Yourself to death for me, and I
Say 'Loved One! take my life, entire; for so,
For You, I want to suffer and to die' . . .

Refrain 1
Yes, You it was who gave the sign
Your words, Lord, '*More no one can do*
Than die for those one loves' enshrine! . . .
    The sovereign Love of mine,
      Jesus, is You!

2   It's late, already it is evening-time;
Come, Lord, and be my Guide upon the way.
This hill that rises, with Your cross I climb:
O Heav'nly Pilgrim, close beside me stay.

Refrain 2
Now echoes of You in me ring:
To be like You is my desire,
So what I ask is suffering:
    Your words blaze up and bring
      In me their fire!

3 You've won Eternal Victory, adored
  By angels, singing of it, joy-immersed:
  To enter, though, into Your Glory, Lord,
  It was appointed that You suffer first!

    Refrain 3
  For *my* sake, on this foreign shore
  You were despised – what hurt You knew!
  So I . . . *last place* I ask You for –
    Wholly to be obscure,
      Jesus, for You!

4 My Loved One, Your example is a call
  To me that I abase myself, despise
  Prestige: enchanting You means staying small –
  So I'll forget myself, to charm Your eyes!

    Refrain 4
  In solitude's my peace, and this
  Is all I ask for. (To pursue
  What pleases You – my study is
    That only!) . . . and my Bliss,
      Jesus, is You.

5 You, Mighty God, whom all the Heav'ns adore,
  You live in *me* – a Prisoner, night and day:
  I always hear Your gentle voice implore –
  'I thirst . . . I thirst for Love' is what You say.

    Refrain 5
  A prisoner – Yours – I shall apply,
  Say over in my turn, to You
  Your tender plea, as Love's reply:
    'O Loved One, Brother – I
      Am thirsting too!'

For Love I thirst! Lord, grant me, by Your touch,
My wishes, for more Fire to warm me by.
For Love I thirst – I suffer very much:
Ah! upward, to my God, I'd like to fly!

Refrain 6
Your Love – my martyrdom of fire,
No other, rises up, and through
Me rings: 'O Jesus, my Desire,
 I ask: make me expire
  For love of You!'

Notes

PN 31

31 May 1896.

The following month – for the second anniversary of her own entry to the Lisieux Carmel – Sr Marie of the Trinity herself composed a short poem which spoke of the 'burning hearth of love' (*brûlant foyer d'amour*) that was Thérèse's heart. Thérèse, that poem says, spends all her life, night and day, in being consumed. Its concluding stanza may be translated as:

> By the contact with her heart's-fire
> A blaze in my own heart is lit
> To consume me! and I aspire
> To the *saving of souls* through it.

'It is because she [Thérèse] considered suffering as the supreme proof of love, as the most adequate way of identifying ourselves with Christ the Saviour, and as the best means of accomplishing God's will to save souls, that she so much desired to suffer.' (Père François Jamart, O.C.D., citing Mgr. Combes).

A word about Sr Marie of the Trinity (Marie-Louise Castel). Her puckish face is easily distinguishable in photographs of the community. She had left the Paris Carmel through ill-health, and seemed to lack emotional stability when she became a novice in Lisieux. Thérèse showed her great affection and recognized her generosity of spirit. She steadied her. This nun's testimony to the diocesan and apostolic tribunals shows admirable maturity.

HEAVEN, THERE FOR ME

1   To bear with exile, in
                        this vale of tears, I need
       The gaze at me, of God
                        the Saviour Whom I love:
       That gaze (it's *full* of love)
                        so charms, that I can read
       Presentiments in me
                        of happiness above.
       I sigh for Jesus: He
                        then smiles . . . and at the sight
       No longer do I feel
                        Faith's trial, for I see
       The Loving Gaze of God,
                        His Smile that's my delight –
       My Heaven, there for me!   ★

2   My Heaven's to attract
                        (a power for that is mine)
       To souls, to Mother Church
                        and all my Sisters here,
       The graces Jesus gives
                        and, ah, His Fire Divine –
       Hearts lighted in that flame
                        rejoice that they are dear!
       All, all, I can obtain
                        from God, Who is my King –
       In talking heart-to-heart,
                        lost in His Mystery;

How sweet, beside the Host
                    the orisons I bring:
            My Heaven, there for me!

3   My Heav'n! To draw forth Life,
                        here to the Host I come;
        For Jesus, there – my Spouse –
                        has veiled Himself. I dare
        To come to where (so small!)
                        my God has made His home –
        He hears me, night and day,
                        my Gentle Saviour there.
        Oh, happy moment when . . .
                        in tenderness He waits! . . .
        He comes to me, that I
                        transformed to Him can be:
        A union of Love
                        that so intoxicates –
            My Heaven, there for me!

4   My Heav'n . . . to sense in me
                        that likeness which will say
        The Mighty Wind of God
                        created me. In this
        My Heaven, *always*, in
                        His presence, I shall stay,
        A child – in calling Him
                        the 'Father' that He is.
        I do not fear the storm,
                        I'm safe in His embrace;
        I've one rule only – that's:
                        'Surrender totally'.

To drowse upon His Heart –
                    the nearness of His Face –
    My Heaven, there for me!

5   My Heav'n . . . the Three-in-One,
                    the Trinity, whose seat
    Is here, within my heart –
                    Love's Prisoner!   Lovingly
    I'll serve You, Captive God,
                    and fearlessly repeat:
    'It's given You outright,
                    the love You have from me.'
    My Heaven is to smile
                    at God, Whom I adore,
    And – when, to test my faith,
                    a Hidden God is He –
    To suffer, *wait* until
                    He'll gaze at me once more . . .
    My Heaven, there for me!

Notes

PN 32

7 June 1896, Feast of Corpus Christi

Written for Sr Vincent de Paul, putting the latter's thoughts into verse.

'. . . when, to test my faith, a Hidden God is He . . .' Thérèse, throughout her writings, uses the metaphors of God 'hiding himself' or 'sleeping' to denote those times (and they were not exceptional) when she had no *emotional* perception of being loved, no feelings of consolation.

To her Spouse, the Son of God Incarnate, she wishes to be the most delicately attentive of spouses. She is humorous, too. She will smile at Him, she says, instead of complaining, and even when He gives the appearance of forgetting her, she will regard that as a compliment: 'He shows me that I am not a stranger by treating me like this.' She is playful, with a spouse's naturalness: 'He will tire more quickly of keeping me waiting than I will of waiting for Him!' (letters to Pauline, January 1889 and May 1890).

★ Last line of each stanza: Lit., 'There is my Heaven, mine.'

MY HOPE

1 Though I am still upon this foreign shore,
I feel the stirrings of a happy state:
Oh, would I were in Heav'n, and that I saw
The marvels that are there to contemplate!
I dream of life eternal – that is when ★
My exile seems no burden! I'm serene:
Soon, God, I'll near my only Home, I then
Will fly to where, before, *I've never been.*

2 O Jesus! give me wings of white, then I
Can come to You, by soaring in the air:
To those Eternal Shores I want to fly –
I want to see You, God my Treasure, there!
I want to fly to Mary's arms – for, near
Her on her throne I'll find such rest in store;
And there she'll give to me, my Mother dear,
The gentle Kiss I've never had before! . . .

3 Loved Jesus! soon, so tenderly (above,
As never yet to me) Your smile impart,
And I, in a delirium of love,
Will (let me!) hide myself inside Your Heart . . .
Oh, happy moment! What a joy to me
To hear You speaking – gently. I'll adore
When first I glimpse Your Face, and in it see
That Glory which I've never seen before . . . .

4   You know, O Sacred Heart of Jesus, why:
        My martyrdom's Your Love, that draws me! For
        If, now, for Heav'n's delightfulness I sigh,
        It's so I'll love You, love You, more and more!
        In Heav'n – as though I'm drunk with love of You
        (No laws, no limits there!) – my happiness
        As first I drank it in, will be, all through
        Eternity, so new . . . and never less!!!

Notes

PN 33

12 June 1896, Feast of the Sacred Heart of Jesus

'Ah . . . I recognize, yes! that all my hopes will be fulfilled . . . yes, the Lord will do marvels for us that will infinitely surpass our *immense desires!'* (Thérèse, letter to Pauline, 28 May 1897).

'. . . I really find it hard to conceive how I will be able to become acclimatized in a country where joy reigns without any mixture of sadness. Jesus will have to transform my soul and give it the capacity for enjoyment, otherwise I shall not be able to bear the eternal delights.' (Thérèse's last letter to Père Roulland, 14 July 1897).

'Never . . . been', etc.: Thérèse's precise words, repeated, are 'for the first time'.

St. 1, l.2 Lit., '. . . sensing eternal happiness.'
★ 'life eternal': Th wrote of eternal 'joys'.

33

THROWING OF FLOWERS

1 Each evening, what a joy
                   when votive-flowers are thrown,
Spring roses . . . as I pull
                   away the petal-leaf,
My only Love! before
                   your Calvary of stone,
     I'd like to wipe away Your grief . . . .

                   Refrain 1
          Throwing of Flowers means 'Gather, straightway bring
All of my lightest sighs
                        and all my deepest woes:
Each little sacrifice –
                   joy, pain, as offering –
     My flowers are those!' . . . .

2 Your beauty, Lord! – my soul's
                   in love! it takes and flings
My perfumes, and my flowers
                   uncounted, to all parts:
In throwing them for You
                   upon the breeze's wings
     I'd like to be enflaming hearts!

Refrain 2

Throwing of Flowers – it arms me, Jesus! I'm
Certain that when I fight
for saving sinners so,
I'll win. By these I can
disarm You every time –
These flowers I throw!!

3   They touch your Face, the flowers;
of this, by their caress –
'My heart is always Yours'
these roses are a sign:
Un-petaled now . . . You know
the thought that they express;
You're smiling at this love of mine.

Refrain 3

Throwing of Flowers, to give you praise once more –
My only pleasure, that,
through all our sad world's hours:
I'll be in Heav'n soon, with
the little angels, for
Throwing of Flowers! . . .

Notes

PN 34

28 June 1896

'I have no other means of proving my love for You than that of throwing flowers, that is, not allowing any little sacrifice to escape, any look, any word; to profit by every little thing and to do it for love.' (*Aut.*, Ms. B)

Every evening during that month of June, Thérèse and the novices collected rose-petals, and, standing in the courtyard, symbolically *flung* them up high, so that some might touch the face of the metal figure of Christ on the granite cross. Can one not just see it? (Their arms go back to give impetus to each long-acred throw.)

TO OUR LADY OF VICTORIES

*Poem originally referring to her spiritual support
for Père Adolphe Roulland, Priest of the Foreign
Missions, who was about to sail for China.
See note below.*

1   To you, my Mother – who obtain
      All that I hope for, I renew
      In love and thanks, my humble strain,
      This heart-song that is sung to you . . . .

2   A missionary's work I share –
      Held fast to it by you, above:
      United, by the bonds of prayer
      And daily suffering, and love.

3   *His* lot's to cross the world, it is
      Proclaiming Jesus. And, for me
      To practise humble virtues: this
      In shadow and in mystery.

4   I ask for suffering: the Cross
      I love – desire! Ah, well you know –
      To save one soul from final loss
      A thousand deaths I'd undergo!

5   A sacrifice, in Carmel, I'd
      Assist in Heaven's conquering –
      Through him, to make flare up inside
      The flames that Jesus came to bring!

6   As into Africa, I'm free   ★[1]
     To journey to the East; I can
     Then make the tender Virgin be
     Loved, as a Mother, in Sut-Chuen!

7   Oh, now in my deep silence may
     I share the work they strive to do!   ★[2]
     Yes, through my brothers, far away,
     I'll be converting sinners too!

8   Through them, baptismal water makes
     A baby of a day become
     A temple! God it is who takes
     In it His loving place – His Home.

9   Through them, what children's legions, I
     Am sure, will up to Heaven rise
     (Angels I want to multiply
     For populating Paradise!)

10   Through them, too, God may now
     The palm for which I really sigh:
     The sister of a Martyr! Oh,
     Dear Mother, how the hope soars high!

11   The glorious battle over – and
     Our exile ended – we, elate,
     Will savour in our Native Land
     The fruits of our apostolate.

12   To them, the victor's crown, before
     The Army of the Blest arrayed.
     To me . . . *their* glory, evermore
     Reflected. It shall never fade.

Notes

PN 35

16 July 1896, Feast of Our Lady of Mount Carmel

'I ask Him that you will be, not only a *good* missionary but a *saint* all on fire with love of God and of souls; I beg you to obtain for me this love also, so that I may be able to help you in your apostolic work. You know that a Carmelite who was not an apostle would be distancing herself from the goal of her vocation and ceasing to be a daughter of the seraphic St Teresa [of Avila] whose desire was to give up a thousand lives to save one soul.' (Thérèse, letter to the Abbé Maurice Bellière, White Fathers seminarian, 21 October 1896).

The Abbé Bellière and Père Roulland were Thérèse's 'spiritual brothers'. She corresponded by letter with both. Each had asked the Lisieux Carmel that one of the nuns support him, from afar, by her prayer and sacrifices.

For a reason that can only be surmised, P reworded this poem so that it appeared to relate to *both* Père Roulland and the Abbé Bellière, but in fact it was written for the former only. In stanzas 7, 8, 9, 10 and 12, the 'they' and 'them' are P's.

St. 4, l. 3 Lit., 'To help to save one soul.'

St. 11, l. 2 'elate', though archaic, *is* in the *Oxford English Dictionary*. It has the meaning of 'elated' and (almost) the sound of 'light'.

★¹ The reference to Africa is wholly P's. It stems from the rewording mentioned above. Sut-Chuen, later in the stanza, alluded to Père Roulland: 'Africa' widened the scope to include the Abbé Bellière!

★² Th wrote that she wanted to 'win hearts', i.e. to gain them for Jesus.

[35]

JESUS ONLY

1   My heart – it needs to prove its tenderness –
Wants to be given *always*, and no less!
To comprehend my love . . . who can keep track?
What heart is there who'll want to pay me back?
Pay back? – my claims aren't met! By none beside
You, Jesus, is my soul's need satisfied.
Nothing could ever charm me here below,
True joy of heart is not encountered so.

> My only peace and heart's reward,
> My only Love, is You, O Lord!

2   Heart-fount of mothers' hearts, Creative Mind!
In You most tender Fatherhood I find.
My Jesus! Word! Your Heart for me in this
Is more maternal than a mother's is.
Always You're here! You guard, You'll never be
Late when I call and ask You 'Come to me';
And if sometimes You seem to hide away,
You come to help me seek You, so to say!

3   Jesus, to only You would I be tied –
It's *Your* arms that I'm rushing to, to hide.
For, like a child's I want my love to be –
And like a warrior, battling valiantly:
Yes – like a dainty child's impulsiveness –
I'll be so lavish, Lord, with my caress,
And, in the field of my apostolate
Launch out myself, a warrior to the fight!

4   You guard one's innocence and make it whole –
Your Heart could not deceive me! In my soul
Is hope in You, that – exile finished – I
Am going to behold You up on high.
When storms of heart upsurge, I raise my head,
Jesus, to You: and it's as though You said
(Your gaze of mercy comes into my view,
Saying): 'My child, I made the Heav'ns for *you*.'

5   I know this very well – my tears and sighs
Are radiant with charm before Your eyes.
You have, as royal court in Heav'n above,
The Seraphim – and yet, You beg *my* love . . . .
You want my heart – it's here! I utterly
Cede my desires to You. Those loved by me
(Jesus, my Spouse and King!) are persons who
Will only now be loved by me *for You*.

Notes

PN 36

15 August 1896, Feast of the Assumption

'Grape-shot, cannon's roar – what does all that matter when one is carried by the General?' (Thérèse, letter to Sr Marie de Saint-Joseph, c. October 1896).

'If the soul wants to live in abandonment, it must not remain at the "level" of the difficulties it meets . . . Instead of battling with temptation or wanting to triumph by itself, the soul immediately rises toward its Father and relies upon Him; better still, it offers the difficulty to Him' (Père Victor de la Vièrge, *op. cit.*): 'It's *Your* arms that I'm rushing to, to hide.'

This poem was written for Sr Marie of the Eucharist and directed towards the latter's excessive entanglement of heart with her family, the Guérins.

In September of this year Thérèse will write Manuscript B: 'I will be love within the heart of the Church . . .'

St. 2, l. 5 'watch and guard' In the French, Thérèse says that at every moment Jesus is *following* and guarding her.

THE SACRISTANS OF CARMEL

1   No job we do could be as nice.
       We tend the altar, and prepare
       The bread and wine: the Sacrifice
       Will give to earth . . . ah, 'Heaven' there!

2   Yes, Heav'n – oh, highest Mystery –
       Which under *bread* has hid away!
       Who *is* this? God Himself! for He   ★
       Comes down to us, and every day.

3   Could ever queenly joy compare
       With that which *our* pursuit allows?
       This job we do – itself a prayer,
       Is one that joins us to our Spouse.

4   Should honours of the world abound
       They'd be as nothing, now, to us
       Who've peace – celestial, profound! –
       Which Jesus makes us savour thus.

5   We bring a holy appetite
       To what our works-of-hand entail,
       Here, as the little Host of white
       Across the Lamb must draw its veil.

6   This, Jesus, Friend and Spouse, inspires
       (Who chose us in His love) to tell:
       That we are hosts and He desires
       To change *us* into Him as well.

7   O Priestly mission, high and grand,
You become *ours* on earth today! –
The Master has transformed us, and
He guides our hearts upon the way.

8   As prayer, as love, is made to count
In what apostles shall have wrought,
Their fields of combat ours, we mount
Our daily fight in their support.

9   This God, whom tabernacle hides –
Our hearts, as well, He's hiding in.
We beg . . . O wonder! He provides
For sinners a release from sin!

10   Our happiness and glory's sum –
To work for Jesus and His goals.
His Heav'n is a ciborium:
We wish to fill it up with souls!

Notes

PN 40

November 1896

In Manuscript B, Thérèse wrote: 'Without doubt, these three privileges are indeed *my vocation, Carmelite, Spouse and Mother*' [of souls]. She then lists other things she felt drawn to ('I feel in me other *vocations*'): WARRIOR, PRIEST, APOSTLE, DOCTOR, MARTYR; 'I feel in me the courage of a Crusader, of a Papal Zouave . . .'

If she were a priest, she muses, 'with what love, O Jesus, I would carry You in my hands when, at my voice, You would come down from Heaven . . . With what love I would give You to souls!' That said, in the next breath she *puts aside such feelings, giving humility as her reason for doing so*: 'But alas! all the time I want to be a *Priest*, I admire and envy the humility of St Francis of Assisi and I feel in me the *vocation* of imitating him in refusing the sublime dignity of *the Priesthood*.' Thérèse cannot be cited in support of the controversialists, the pressure groups.

Four years before she had written: '. . . our mission as Carmelites is to form those labourers in the Gospel who will save thousands of souls, whose mothers we shall be . . . I find our portion very beautiful, what have we to envy in priests?' (letter to Céline, 15 August 1892).

Thérèse's words in stanza 7, lit., 'Sublime mission of the Priest, you become ours [the nun-sacristans'] here below are a devotional analogy or metaphor. She poetically represents the sacristans as altar-breads (stanza 6) 'transformed by the Divine Master' (stanza 7).

St. 5, l. 1 'appetite': Thérèse uses the word *envie*, 'desire' or 'longing'.

★ This, by contrast with stanza 1, refers to the time *after* the Consecration in the Mass. Th in fact wrote, 'Heaven is Jesus Himself'.

37

STILL A SONG OF LOVE

1   Jesus, my God, I'm praying now to tell
    My fervent love for You. I would impart
    Delight to You alone (You know this well –
    Oh, grant the ardent longing of my heart!).
    I'll bear the sorrows of this exile, for   ★[1]
    That is a way to charm and comfort You! –
    Change into Love (O Saviour, I implore)
    Each little daily task that here I do.

2   Yours, Jesus, is the Love that I desire!
    It's that which must transfigure me, for when
    You fill my heart with Your consuming fire . . .
    Do that, and I can bless and love You then!
    I'm very poor; yet love that's worth the name   ★[2]
    I'll love You with, as those in Heaven do:
    Yes, Jesus! with such Love – the very same –
    As I received, O Son of God, from You.

3   My God and Master, at my dying breath
    May I be gazing up to Heav'n above.   ★[3]
    Reveal to me Your tenderness in death
    By one bright ray of Your Eternal Love!   ★[4]
    Oh, that Your gentle voice will call to me
    And say 'I am your Saviour: come, depart   ★[5]
    From there, my faithful dove, fly up and be
    Reposing in this nest, my lovesome Heart!'   ★[6]

Notes

PN 41

End of 1896

'I understood that there were many degrees of perfection and that each soul was free to respond to the advances of Our Lord, to do little or much for Him, in a word, to *choose* among the sacrifices He asks. Then, as in the days of my babyhood, I cried out: "My God, *I choose all!*" I don't want to be a *saint by halves . . .*' (Ms. A).

Poem written at the request of Sr Saint-Jean de la Croix.

P re-worded this poem more than any other.

★[1] 'sorrows' (*misères*) is P's word. Th's wording carried overtones of life as a testing-time.
★[2] The reference to poverty (*indigence*) is P's.
★[3] 'May I be gazing up' is P's. Th's wording begged that Jesus come and seek her immediately on death.
★[4] 'ray' is a metaphor added by P.
★[5] 'I am your Saviour' is a phrase of P's substituted for Th's wording which made Jesus assure her of *pardon*.
★[6] A bird to its nest, a lover to her Beloved. It is P who introduces the former image.

38

TO THE CHILD JESUS

*Thérèse imagines herself in a boat
with the Holy Child.*

1   Ah, Jesus! my name you know;
     Your loving gaze at me here
     Says 'Your worries on *Me* throw,
     Just that, it is I who'll steer!'

2   With little voice uplifted, You
               Can quiet the sea –
     O marvel! . . . winds uproaring, too
     I've heard Your little voice subdue
               As they blew.

3   If you want to rest and stay
     As the thunder-rumbles scold –
     Upon me, I beg you! lay
     Your head's little fringe of gold.

4   How sweet your smile in sleep! And who
               Is there who would be
     Not moved to sing what I've in view . . .
     Tenderly as one's able to,
               Rocking you.

Notes

PN 42

December 1896

'My Céline . . . is . . . in a small boat, *land* has disappeared from her sight . . . the helm, which Céline cannot even glimpse, is not without a pilot. Jesus is there, *sleeping* as once He did in the boat of the Galilean fishermen . . . The wind blows . . . yet if He awoke, but for an instant, He would have only to "command the wind and the sea" . . . The apostles have given Him a *pillow* . . . But in His dear *bride's* little boat Our Lord finds another pillow much softer; it is Céline's *heart* . . .' (Thérèse, letter to Céline, 23 July 1893).

The parallels between the letter and the poem are strong. But in the poem Jesus – strong helmsman there, as in the letter – is the Child of Bethlehem. Paradox of the Incarnation!

St. 3, l. 2 'thunder-rumbles scold': Thérèse's verb *gronder*, scold, also describes what thunder does; it rumbles or growls.

39

THE AVIARY OF
THE CHILD JESUS

1   For exiles here, His love to show,
     God made the birds whose chirping fills –
     Birds *pray* so, going to and fro –
     The valleys and the sides of hills.

2   Joyfully, flighty children choose
     The ones they like, and then they hold
     Them prisoners in cages – whose
     Bars have been painted all in gold.

3   Our Little Brother thus to be,
     Jesus! You quitted Paradise.   ★¹
     And, Holy Child, Your aviary –
     Carmel, of course, that signifies!

4   Though *our* cage isn't golden, we
     Are fond of it, and by His grace
     We never hanker to be free
     To seek the woods, the azure space.

5   In this world's groves find our content?
     There, Jesus, we're not able to!
     Through hours in deep seclusion spent –
     Thus we would sing, and just for You.

6   Your little hand, dear Child – it takes
     Our hearts . . . ah, how your charms endear!
     And, Jesus – God – your *smile!* It makes
     The little birds your captives here.

7 The soul, in its simplicity,
    Finds here the object of its love.
    The vulture will no longer be
    The terror of the timid dove.

8 One sees it – on the wings of prayer
    The ardent heart is soaring high,
    As when the lark – in upper air –
    Sings as it rises in the sky.

9 What song – as in their cage they stay –
    From wren and merry chaffinch pours!
    O little Jesus, listen: they
    Chirp out Your name, these birds of Yours!

10 The little bird, on singing bent –
    No troubles for his food appear: ★²
    A grain of millet – he's content!
    He never has to sow it here.

11 And to *our* aviary You bring
    All that we need! What we've to do –
    The only necessary thing,
    O God and Child! is loving You.

12 As well, we sing Your praises: so
    With those pure-spirits up above
    Unite. The birds of Carmel know
    The Angels look at them, and love!

13 Jesus, to wipe away Your tears
    (Which sinners cause) Your birds repeat
    Their song – about Your charms! One hears
    Them gain You hearts by singing sweet.

14   From this sad world, one happy day
      You'll call them! Through the aviary door
      That's opened now, they'll fly away:
      All of them, up to Heaven soar.

15   In Heaven's heights, we'll fly among
      The joyous little cherubim:
      And greet the Child Divine! The song
      We'll sing then is in praise of Him.

Notes

PN 43

Christmas 1896

'From the time of my departure from the boarding school, I installed myself in *Pauline's* old painting-room and arranged it to my taste. It was a real bazaar, a collection of pious objects and curiosities, a garden and an aviary . . . I had a table on which was placed a *large cage*, containing a *large* number of birds, whose melodious song deafened the ears of visitors, but not those of their little mistress who cherished them very much . . .' (Thérèse at Les Buissonnets: Ms. A).

'Immensity will be our domain . . . we shall no longer be prisoners in this land of exile . . . *everything* will have PASSED!' (Thérèse, letter to Céline, 12 March 1889).

★¹ 'quitted': Th had the present tense; the poem was written for
     Christmas.
★² 'for his food': Th wrote of 'his life', a wider and more luminous
     concept.

[40]

TO MY LITTLE BROTHERS
IN HEAVEN, THE HOLY INNOCENTS

*There is perhaps a secondary allusion to
her own two sisters and two brothers who
died in infancy.*

1   O happy Little Ones! –

          ah, with what tenderness
        Did Heaven's King
Bless you! He on your brows –

          to joy you – His caress
        Was lavishing!
(All Innocents do you,

          in figure, comprehend);
        Reflection brings
A glimpse of what in Heav'n

          You're giving, without end,
        O King of kings.

2   Such riches you have seen

          (dear little Lilies), there
        In Paradise –
Before you've had to know

          the wretchedness *we* share,
        You've won the prize!
O scented buds the Lord

          has gathered from the hour
        Of morning dew,

What gentle Sun of Love
                    knew how to make you flower? –
        His Heart: It knew.

3   Such *care* does Mother Church
                            (in honouring your birth,
                Your death) display!
        What tenderness of joy,
                        for you whose life on earth
                Was but a day . . .
        For – in her Mother's arms;
                            first fruits of Harvest – so
                She offered you
        To God: and what delights,
                            eternally, you'll know
                In Heaven's blue!

4   You, virginal, the Lamb
                            accompany and praise:
                O Children, we
        May hear you singing there
                            (an honour to amaze)
                New melody!
        O conquerors, you've won
                        strange glory that without
                Combat occurs!
        For you the Saviour put
                        the enemy to rout,
                Sweet vanquishers!

5   No precious stones your hair

                    illuming, does one see
         The Heavens hold:
Reflected – a delight
                of silkiness! – will be
         Your locks of gold . . . .
The palms, the crowns that are
                the treasures of the Blest –
         You have all these . . .
And, children, in your Home
                rich thrones: you take your rest
         Upon *their knees.*

6   About the Altar with

                the cherubim at play
         You now belong:
A graceful troop! as you're
                enchanting Heav'n that way
         With children's song.
The Good Lord tells you how
                He makes the winds, the rose,
         The birds; and so
No genius on earth,
                O Little Children, knows
         What you all know! . . .

7   The secrets that behind

                the azure veils retire
         You now behold:
Into your little hands
                you take the stars (like fire –
         A thousandfold) . . . .

You, running, often mark
                          with trace of silver ray
            The evening air:
I think that when I gaze
                          upon the Milky Way
            I see you there!

8   And after all your fun
                          you rush to Mary's arms,
            And she will keep
Within her starry veil
                          those golden heads . . . . She calms
            You all to sleep.
O charming little imps,
                          how boldly you embrace
            The Lord (and this
So pleases Him): you dare –
                          He lets you – stroke His Face:
            How kind He is!

9   O Innocents, to try
                          on earth to be as *small* –
            That I will do.
To be a child! . . . the Lord
                          asks me to mirror all
            That's seen in you.
Help me! – those charming things
                          which in a child one sees:
            Your openness,
Your lovely innocence,
                          your total trust – all these
            May I possess!

10   Lord, well You know I burn
                 for what, in exile, to
         My soul is dear:
      And, Lily of the Vale,
                 I'd gather up for You
         Bright lilies here.
      To please You – that is why
                 I cherish, and look for
         These buds of Spring:
      I beg You, upon them
                 Baptismal water pour: ★
         Come garnering! . . .

11   O Innocents! may now
                 your troop yet wider range;
         Because my goal's
      To add to it – my joys,
                 my sorrows, in exchange
         For children's souls!
      Among these Innocents
                 I beg to have a place,
         King of the Blest:
      And, Jesus! then, like them,
                 to kiss Your gentle Face
         And be caressed.

Notes

PN 44

28 December 1896, Feast of the Holy Innocents

'. . . ah! don't be afraid to tell Him that you *love Him, even though you have no feeling of love*; that is the way to *force* Jesus to come to your aid, to carry you like a little child too weak to walk.' (Thérèse, letter to Sr Marthe, c. June 1897).

'The Holy Innocents will not be little children in Heaven; they will have only the indefinable charms of childhood. They are represented as "children" because we have a need of pictures to understand spiritual things' (*Last Conversations*, 21. 26 May 1897).

It is necessary not to be put off by Thérèse's use of childish expressions and imagery: they cover solid spiritual doctrine. 'To be a child! . . .' (St. 9), in humility and confidence, is central.

★ Th's word-image was of the watering of lilies by the *dew* of Baptism.

MY PEACE AND MY JOY! ★

1   Happiness – people search for it;
With no success the hunt is crowned.
For me, it's quite the opposite,
Here in my heart *is* joy – it's found!
Not like a flower that blooms and goes,
Coming to me, it came to stay.
Delighting, like a fresh spring rose,
It smiles upon me every day.

2   Truly! I'm far too happy, for
It's my own will I always do . . . .
How could I *not* be joyous, or
Not let my gaiety show through?
My joy's from love of suffering,
And, though with tears these eyes are blind,
I smile. I'm truly welcoming
Thorns with the flowers intertwined.

3   When Heaven's blue grows dark, and so
Seems to have left me cast aside,
My joy's to see myself brought low –
To stay within the shade, to hide.
My peace, His Holy Will (so dear
Is Jesus!) – *that* I shall obey.
And so I live devoid of fear:
I love the night as much as day.

4   My peace comes from my staying small;
     And when I trip upon a stone,
     I get up quick. For when I fall
     He takes my hand into His own!
     Then, cov'ring Him with my caress,
     To Jesus: 'You're my All' I say.
     I give Him twice the tenderness
     When, from my Faith, He slips away.

5   If, sometimes, tears pour out – it's been
     My joy that I've been hiding those.
     To give my suff'ring *charm*, between
     A veil of flowers I interpose!
     To suffer, silently, so I'll
     Give Jesus comfort – that's my will.
     My joy comes when I see Him smile,
     Though I am here in exile still.

6   My peace . . . is striving that I'll bring
     Children of Heav'n to birth; it is
     A heart aflame, and whispering
     Over to Jesus, often, this:
     'For You (small Brother and Divine!)
     I'll suffer; I am happy to.
     The only earthly joy of mine –
     That I can give delight to You.

7   'Long as I want my life to be
     If that's what You desire, yet, too –
     If it would please You, this from me,
     To Heav'n I'd like to follow You.
     Love's ceaseless fire consumes, from where
     My soul has Home – in Heav'n above.
     It's death? it's life? – I do not care!
     My only joy's to give You love.'

Notes

PN 45

21 January 1897, Feast of St Agnes

'*Wood* is not within our reach when we are in darkness, in dryness, but are we not at least obliged to throw on small bits of straw? Jesus is indeed powerful enough to keep the fire going by Himself, yet He is glad when He sees us putting on a little fuel; that is a *delicate attention* that pleases Him, and then He throws much wood on the fire . . .'

'. . . when I *feel* nothing . . . then is the moment to look for small opportunities . . . for example, a smile, a friendly word when what I would like to do is to say nothing or wear a bored look, etc. etc. . . . When I have no (such) opportunities, at least I wish to tell Him often that I love Him; that isn't difficult and it keeps the *fire* going. *Even though* it seemed to me that this fire of love had gone out, I would want to throw something on it, and Jesus would then well know how to relight it' (Thérèse, letter to Céline, 18 July 1893).

St. 5, l. 4 'A veil of flowers': a smile. She will not let her suffering show.

★ Th's title was 'My Joy'. P made it read 'My Peace and My Joy'; and in three instances (stanzas 3, 4 and 6) she changed Th's 'joy' to 'peace'. Perhaps this was simply to avoid what she saw as an infelicitous repetition of 'joie'; but see also page xxviii of Translator's Introduction. Th retained her joy, peace, even when (as at the time this poem was written) she was in great darkness of soul.

42

TO MY GUARDIAN ANGEL

1   Glorious Guardian of my soul,
You – shining one – in Heaven fly:
Pure flame! your gentle aureole
Burns by the Throne of God on high.
You come to earth *for me*, and how
You light me here! For you descend,
Fair Angel, as my Brother now.
You are my Comforter and Friend.

2   Knowing how weak I am, you take
My hand, and on the road ahead,
Tenderly watchful for my sake,
You clear the stones from where I tread.
You put to me . . . you gently call
For Heaven *only* to enchant –
The more I'm humble and am small,
The more your face is radiant!

3   O spirit who can tráverse space
More quick than sheets of lightning do!
Fly very often, in my place,
To be beside my dear ones too.
Dry, with your wing, their tears – and sing
How good is Jesus; and proclaim
That there is charm in suffering!
And murmur, very low . . . my name.

4   For saving sinners (as I so
                Desire to, short as life may be –
                Fair Angel, they're my brothers) – oh,
                Your holy ardours give to me!
                I've here my sacrifices, and –
                I've nothing more – my poverty:
                With all your bliss in Heaven's Land,
                Offer them to the Trinity.

5   To you: the wealth of Endless Light
                The King of kings has empire at.
                To me: the humble Host of white,
                To me, the Cross – a treasure that!
                The Cross, the Host – ah yes, with these
                And with the aid I thank you for,
                I'll wait the other life, in peace –
                Its joys, that last for evermore.

Notes

PN 46

January 1897

Thérèse 'had a devotion to the holy angels and particularly to her guardian angel whom she loved to invoke often' (Sr Marie of the Trinity, deposition, 1916).

For all the purity and power of angels (e.g. stanza 3, lines 1–2), in Thérèse's eyes they lack two great prerogatives which human beings have: as pure spirits they cannot suffer, and they cannot die as martyrs (cf. Poem 3). 'The angels cannot suffer, they are not as happy as I am', Thérèse remarked, a month before her death.

43

TO THE VENERABLE
THÉOPHANE VÉNARD

*Priest of the Foreign Missions, martyred 1861
in Tonkin (Vietnam), aged 31.
Canonised, 1988.*

1   Now all the Blest in Heav'n sing out your praise,
Théophane, *Martyr* – like an Angel, too!
Seraphim (thinking of your earthly days)
In angel-hosts, aspire to serving you!
I'm still in exile here, I cannot pour
My voice out with the Blest as I desire:
At least, however, on this arid shore,
To sing your virtues now, I take my lyre.

2   That hymn was sweet, *your* exile. (It was short,
But how you captured hearts by what you'd say!).
For Jesus, your poetic spirit brought
The ground to blossom where you took your way.
And as your soul was going up at death
Your leaving-song was still as fresh as Spring:
You murmured 'Short this life of mine, a breath;
I'm "going first", to Paradise I wing!'

3   O Happy Martyr! at the torture's height,
In suffering, you *savoured* what befell:
You – suffering for God was a delight –
Knew, smiling, how to die and live as well!
Your slaughterer – should he accelerate
Your death? he asked – straightway your answer had:

'The longer is my martyrdom, more great
Its value, and the more I shall be glad !!!'

4   O Virgin Lily! in your Springtime days
      The King heard your desires and answered them –
      You were a bloom, of whitest fire ablaze:
      The Lord desired to pick you off the stem.
      You now (no longer in our exiled state –
      Full open) plaudits from the Blessèd win!
      The Virgin – Rose of Love, Immaculate –
      Has smelled your perfume and has breathed it in.

5   Soldier of Christ! Lend *me* your arms! that, for
      The souls of sinners I may fight. I long
      To shed my tears, my blood, in holy war –   ★¹
      Protect me! Help me! so that I'll be strong.
      These battles, in an endless fight – they form
      Assaults upon the Kingdom! For my aim –
      For sinners' sake – is taking it by storm:
      Not peace the Lord brought us, but Sword and Flame!

6   How dear this faithless shore-line – in the way
      It was the object of *your* ardent love:
      And if my Jesus asked me to, one day
      I'd happily return there from above.
      Before Him, though, no distances: all things
      The universe contains – a pinpoint these!
      My feeble love, my little sufferings
      Can make Him loved, and right across the seas.   ★²

7   Ah! may the Lord soon see me, too, as a flower –
      A flower of Spring He'll gather *soon,* then you
      May come down here to me, at my last hour –
      O Blessèd Martyr, I beseech you to!

And, from your love, your purity that glows,
May I, on earth, be set alight by you!
Then I can fly up Heavenwards, with those
Who'll make up your eternal retinue!

Notes

PN 47

2 February 1897, thirty-sixth anniversary of Théophane Vénard's martyrdom.

'One light blow from a sabre will separate my head from my body, like a Spring flower which the Master of the garden picks for his pleasure' (Théophane, letter before his execution).

Jesus 'willed to create great saints who could be compared to lilies and roses, but He has also created smaller ones . . . Perfection consists in doing His will, in being what He wants us to be' (*Aut.*, Ms. A).

'I know that St Thérèse is known everywhere as the Little Flower and that it was the name she gave herself. It is no doubt presumptuous of me to say that I do not care for it . . . It is a phrase which can create a very false image of her.' Thérèse's character 'was more like an oak tree than a little flower. Her will was of steel.' (John Beevers, Introduction to his translation of Thérèse's autobiography).

St. 2, l. 8 Days before his execution, Théophane wrote to his father: 'Little ephemeral one that I am, I am going first.'

★¹ 'shed my tears, my blood' is P's. Th referred to Théophane, victorious in heaven.

★² Th adds 'Blessed by Him', i.e. God.

44

MY ARMS

1   From the Almighty I have taken arms;
I've been arrayed in them by God above!
Nothing now on, for me, will cause alarms –
For who could ever part me from His Love?
Come sword or fire, next *Him* I'll stay serene –
I'll rush to the arena fearlessly;
My enemies will know I am a queen –
      A spouse of God is what they'll see!
Jesus, I'll guard this armour, that I don
In adoration (which Your eyes arouse):
My exile's end, and still . . .
              my loveliest garments on! –
      These are my sacred Vows.

2   Poverty – my first sacrifice! you'll be
Companion till my earthly life is done.
It's like an athlete in the Games – when he
Is totally detached . . . *then* he can run!
Taste, wordly ones (for it's remorse and pain)
The bitter produce of your vanity.
In the arena is my joy and gain;
      See there my palms – in Poverty!
'By violence does one take and bear away
The Kingdom' (in the Gospel Jesus said):
Well, Poverty will be
              the Lance of my array,
      The Helmet on my head.

3   Chastity makes me kin to angels, who –
     In purity have gained their victory.
     To soar with them one day, I've this to do
     (I, too) – on earth, some fighting's due from me!
     Yes, fight I must, no rest or truce! Record –
     The Lord of lords, my Spouse, I'm fighting for –
     That Chastity (for it's my Heav'nly Sword)
             Of hearts for Him, is conqueror!
     Chastity arms me. It, invincible,
     Makes all my foes give in to me and fly:
     And by it I become . . .
                     joy inexpressible! –
                 Jesus's Spouse am I.

4   Lucifer – pride-possessed in all his light –
     Still has as blazon 'I will not obey!'
     I blazon, to light up the earthly night:
     'I'll be obedient, always' – *that* I say!
     A holy daring's born in me: elate,
     I'll brave the whole of hell and never yield!
     Obedience – my strength and armour-plate –
             Is, for my heart, a solid Shield.
     That glory only, God of Hosts! My will
     Submissive to You, wholly – that's my plea:
     Since one who has obeyed
                     can tell his victories still
                 Throughout Eternity!

5   If with a warrior's power-in-arms I fight,
     And if like him I struggle valiantly,
     Yet, too, like her whose grace is our delight,
     The Virgin – I would strive, but sing as she!
     You make the strings upon this lyre vibrate
     (This heart within me, Jesus – it's Your lyre!)

                     [159]

To sing of how Your Mercies are so great –
    Sing of their gentleness and fire.
So, smiling, I will face the bullets' hail –
    My Spouse! . . . ah, how Your comfort of me calms!
I'll die upon the field
              still singing! – for still they'll
        Be held by me, those Arms!

Notes

PN 48

25 March 1897, Feast of the Annunciation

Thérèse of Lisieux 'is fearless . . . She loves *war*. She is a fighter by nature' (Hans Urs von Balthasar, *Thérèse of Lisieux*).

'I made you smile, dear little Brother, in singing of "My Arms"; well, I am going to make you smile again by telling you that when I was a child I dreamt of fighting on battlefields . . . (but) instead of a voice from Heaven inviting me to the fight [like Joan of Arc] I heard in the depths of my soul a voice sweeter and stronger still . . . I understood that my mission was, not to get a mortal being crowned but the King of Heaven loved; to make subject to Him the realm of hearts' (Thérèse, letter to the Abbé Bellière, 25 April 1897).

This poem was written for Marie Guérin (Sr Marie of the Eucharist) on the occasion of her Profession.

45

TO OUR LADY OF PERPETUAL SUCCOUR

1   Since I was young, of course, your picture here
Has given me delight of heart; I knew –
Seeing you look at me – you held me dear:
My happiness was being close to you.

Refrain
     I'll go and see *you* – always! – when I quit
     This foreign shore, O Mary. Ah, but how
         Good that your picture's here, for it
         Is my Perpetual Succour – now!

2   When I was well-behaved, obedient,
You seemed to smile at me: but I would see,
If sometimes I was naughty . . . well, that meant
I thought I saw you crying over me.

3   In granting what I simply asked you to,
A loving Mother, always you would show
To me – I found this when I looked at you –
A little taste of Heaven, here below.

4   I feel you make me strong, dear Mother, when
I'm fighting for my God with battle-sword:
You know that, at the close of life . . . ah, then
I'd like to offer *Priests* up to the Lord!

5   O picture, of my Mother up on high,
You'll be my joy for ever – for you will
For ever be my treasure . . . . Oh! may I
In my last moments gaze upon you still.

Last refrain
O Mary, I shall sit upon your knee –
At death I shall have flown up to your feet:
All to myself, you'll give to me
Your kisses, Mother – ah, so sweet!

Notes

PN 49

March 1897

'What I came to do in Carmel I declared at the feet of Jesus-the-Host, in the examination which preceded my profession: "I have come to save souls, and above all in order to pray for priests"' (*Aut.*, Ms. A).

The picture referred to in this poem is that of Our Lady of Perpetual Succour (or 'Perpetual Help'). This ancient picture, Byzantine in style, is now in the Church of St Alphonsus Liguori in Rome. It represents the Blessed Virgin holding the Divine Child; the archangels Michael and Gabriel present before Him the Cross and other instruments of His Passion. Renewed devotion to Our Lady under that title was fostered by the Redemptorist Fathers in the nineteenth century.

Thérèse had a facsimile of this picture in her breviary. Sr Marie of the Trinity (for whom this poem was written) felt a great attraction to the picture. She entered the Lisieux Carmel on the eve of the Feast of Our Lady of Perpetual Succour 1894, overcoming previous difficulties after praying to the Virgin under that title. She, Sr Marie, is the 'I' in the poem.

This translation, except for one word, is from the version published in *La Sainte Famille*, Paris, in May 1934.

St. 4, l. 2 Thérèse simply says 'When I fight . . . In the combat'.

46

AN UN-PETALED ROSE

1   First, Jesus, Mary's hands
                    made sure you didn't fall:
             Then, on your own,
     You tried, on this sad earth,
                    shakily first of all
             To walk alone . . .
     Before You, I would break
                    the petals off a rose
             Fresh from the bower –
     So that each little foot
                    of Yours, that forward goes
             Treads on a flower! . . .

2   This rose, *un-petaled now*,
                    is, Holy Child! that heart
             (The figure's true)
     Which wants to immolate
                    itself – in every part,
             Always, for You.
     Fresh altar-roses, Lord,
                    are gratified to shine –
             Self-gifts we *see*! –
     Instead of that *I* would
                    (this other dream is mine)
             Un-petal me . . .

3 Delightful Child! the rose
         can deck Your Feast-days when
     It's at its height.
  The rose, *un-petaled* though –
         thrown to the wind's will, then
     On, out of sight!
  That rose gives up itself –
         all artless – that it may
     No longer live.
  Child Jesus! I, to You
         give *my*self up that way –
     Joyously give!

4 Upon these petals now
         one walks without regret:
     And their debris
  Are ornaments by no
         deliberation set –
     That I quite see.
  For You, I've strewn my life –
         my future, with what's gone:
     To mortal eye,
  A rose that always will
         be withered from now on,
     I ought to *die*!

5 Supremely lovely Child!
         for You I ought to die –
     Happily too!
  I'll die to show You I,
         un-petaled, love You . . . my
     Heart's-love is You . . .

Beneath Your infant steps
                    I'll live, while here below,
        In mystery:
I'll soften, too, Your steps –
                    Your last ones, those that go
        To Calvary!

Notes

PN 51

19 May 1897

By this month it was clear that Thérèse was gravely ill. Her weakness and her pain were to become worse. She now had only four months to live.

'It isn't "death" that will come and seek me, it's the good God. Death is not a phantom, a horrible spectre, as represented in pictures. It says in the catechism that "death is the separation of the soul and the body", that's all it is!' (*Last Conversations*, 1 May 1897).

Her illness advancing, Thérèse expresses in this poem a complete surrender of being and of will to God. She wants only what will please Him. When she was approaching fifteen (she had written in the autobiography) she had, for some time then, offered herself 'to the Child Jesus as His *little plaything* . . . a little ball of no value' that He could do what He liked with (Ms. A).

In the following month, June, she will be ordered by Mère Gonzague to continue her autobiography by writing what became Manuscript C.

St. 3, ll. 7–8 Lit., 'Like it [the rose], I happily surrender myself to You, little Jesus.'

St. 4, l. 5 'For You': lit., 'For Your love', 'for love of You' (*pour ton amour*).

47

SURRENDER'S THE DELICIOUS FRUIT OF LOVE

*'Surrender' – L'abandon – means self-surrender,
total abandonment of oneself to the
Will of God.*

1.
There is on earth a Tree
That bears a wondrous fruit;
That grows . . . O mystery! –
In Heaven is its root.

2.
Its shade will never fail
To keep one safe from harm.
One will not fear the gale –
For, there, one can be calm.

3.
And from its branches fair
(The tree is Love) there came
A fruit, that's sweet and rare –
Surrender is its name.

4.
In life, this fruit divine
Has given me content –
Such joy of heart is mine
At so divine a scent!

5.
This fruit's a treasure when
I touch it on the tree:
But tasting it! ah, then
It's sweeter still for me.

6   It gives me, here below,
    Repose – a sea of peace;
    Unfathomable, so
    That it will never cease.

7   Surrender! It will give
    Me to Your arms, to rest:
    That, only, makes me live
    Nourished as are the Blest.

8   Surrendering to You –
    O Spouse Divine! – I'll raise
    My eyes: for I pursue
    Only *Your* gentle gaze.

9   Upon Your Heart I'd stay,
    To drowse with my Adored . . .
    I'll smile, and simply say
    To You, 'I love You, Lord.'

10 A daisy, to the sky
    Looks up (red-chaliced one).
    A *little* flowerlet, I
    Half-open to the Sun.

11 My gentle Sun – You shine,
    O lovely King! – is You
    Who are the Host Divine:
    You've become little too.

12 Your Flame of Sun – as coal
    Sends out a blaze of heat –
    Gives light, and in my soul
    Surrender is complete.

13   If creatures *all* desert
                      Me – well, I'll let them do!
                      In that, there'll be no hurt
                      When I am near to You.

14   If You desert me (O,
                      My Treasure! God) I will –
                      Deprived of sweetness – show
                      You I am smiling still.

15   In peace, I will await
                      Your coming-back, my King –
                      Not by a note abate
                      The hymns of love I sing.

16   No, Jesus! I have got
                      No fear of woes-to-be –
                      Even the lark can not
                      Fly higher up than me.

17   Dark clouds? If one could soar
                      Through them, it's blue above! –
                      One lands upon the shore
                      Where reigns the God of Love.

18   I wait in *peace,* to come
                      To Heaven as an heir.
                      See, this ciborium –
                      The Fruit of Love is there!

Notes

PN 52

31 May 1897

'Holiness does not consist in this or that practice. It consists in a *disposition of the heart*, which makes us humble and little in the arms of God, well aware of our feebleness, but boldly confident in the Father's goodness': Thérèse (*Novissima Verba*).

Sr Thérèse de Saint-Augustin (see note to Poem 1) asked Thérèse, ill but not yet in the infirmary, to write a poem about *abandon*. On publication of the poem after Thérèse's death, its title was attributed to that other Thérèse's patron, St Augustine.

St. 3 In this stanza Thérèse calls the tree *ineffable* – 'indescribable', beyond description.

St. 10, l. 3 The French also has a double diminutive ('*petite* fleurette', italicized thus).

St. 12, l. 1 This is a free translation. Thérèse (who elsewhere speaks of a 'hearth of love') here does not mention coal, only fire.

48

A LILY IN THE MIDST
OF THORNS

For, and about, Sister Marie of the Trinity

1 Lord, You have chosen me ' and since my childhood days;
Yes, I can call myself ' a work-of-love of Yours.
Would I could pay You back ' in gratitude and praise,
In giving thanks for that ' of which You were the cause!
Poor nothing that I am, ' what have I done for You
(Loved Jesus!) that You give ' me honour of this sort?
And now I find I've joined ' the white-clad retinue –
My God and Beauteous King, ' the virgins of Your court!

2 I'm feebleness itself, ' and nothing more, I fear!
You know it, O my God; ' and yet . . . You know this too –
I have no virtues, yet ' my most-Beloved here
Who's captivated me ' – my Jesus, that *is You*!
When that in my young heart ' was lighted, like a flame
(The name of it is love) ' You asked for it from me:
And, Jesus, only You ' could satisfy my claim,
My soul had such a need ' to love – and endlessly!

3 When, like a little lamb, ' I'd frolic, and would fail
To heed, beyond the fold, ' the dangers that are there,
Then, Queen of Heav'n, you'd make ' me safe inside the vale –
Unseen, you'd show to me ' a Shepherdess's care.
And even when I played ' beside a precipice,
You lifted – even then ' my eyes to Carmel's heights.
To fly to Heaven! . . . first ' (I comprehended this)
What I would have to love ' were these austere delights.

4   Yet, if You cherish, Lord, [|] such purity of fire
As Angel spirits show [|] who ride the air above,
Do You not cherish, too [|] – uplifted from the mire –
The lily You keep pure [|] and holy by Your love?
If *he* is happy, God, [|] the angel as he soars
On his vermilion wings [|] before You – pure to see,
Here, Angel! on the earth [|] my joy's the same as yours,
Such treasure I have now, [|] in my virginity!

Notes

PN 53

May 1897

'You want news of [Marie Castel, later Sr Marie of the Trinity, to whom Thérèse was acting as assistant novice-mistress] . . . I really believe she WILL STAY . . . (Thérèse, letter to Céline, 18 July 1894).

[49]

WHY I LOVE YOU, MARY!

1 O Mary, I would sing ' '*I love you – this is why*';
 It's why your gentle name ' brings flutters to my heart,
 And why the thought of all ' your grandeur up on high
 Could never, to my soul ' a second's fear impart.
 If I should gaze on you ' in glory and perceive
 A blaze that all the saints' ' – all their lights – multiplies,
 That I'm a child of yours ' I then could scarce believe –
 Before you, Mary, *then* ' I'd lower dazzled eyes!

2 A mother (that she'll be ' then lovable the more)
 Must share her small one's griefs ' – *weep*, even, with him too!
 O Queen who rules my heart! ' upon this foreign shore,
 Ah, how your many tears ' attract *this* child to you . . .
 For when *your life, as in* ' *the Gospel*, I recall,
 I dare to look, and then ' approach the one I see:
 Believing I'm your child's ' not difficult at all;
 I see you – mortal, and ' you're suffering like me . . .

3 When Heaven's angel came ' to offer you no less
 Than *Motherhood* of God ' (whose reign's eternal) . . . see!
 You, Mary you preferred ' – what words cannot express –
 The treasure, kept for Him, ' of your *Virginity*.
 O Spotless Virgin, I ' see this: you wouldn't fail
 To be more dear to Him ' than His Abode above:
 Your soul that can contain ' (*Low-lying, gentle Vale*)
 Your Jesus – even He, ' that Ocean-flood of Love! . . .

4   I love you, whom I call ˈ the little servant-maid ★[1]
Of God, whom you delight ˈ by your humility –
Hid virtue, which gives you ˈ almightiness . . . arrayed
By this your heart attracts ˈ the Blessed Trinity!
God's Holy Spirit, Love ˈ *came down, and in His shade*
The Father's equal Son ˈ *. . . becomes your little one!*
So many sinners were ˈ to be His brothers made,
Jesus, we have to say, ˈ became your first-born Son!

5   Ah! Mary, this you know: ˈ despite my littleness,
That same Almighty *I* ˈ possess in me, like you.
I see my weakness, but ˈ it gives me no distress –
'A mother's treasure' means ˈ her child has treasure too.
I am your child indeed, ˈ O Mary! Mother dear;
Your virtues and your love ˈ are they not mine? and when
The Host of white comes down ˈ to rest in my heart here,
Your Lamb believes he comes ˈ to you – to *your* heart then!

6   It's you who make me feel ˈ it really can be done –
To follow you, O Queen ˈ of all the Saints! Ahead
The narrow road to Heav'n ˈ you've made a well-lit one:
In daily little things – ˈ I see the path you tread.
O Mary, next to you, ˈ I love my staying small;
Of great things here below ˈ I see the vanity.
Your Visitation to ˈ your Cousin I recall
And learn to imitate ˈ your ardent charity!

7   I listen, on your knee ˈ O gentle Queen of Heav'n – ★[2]
That sacred song your heart ˈ pours out has now begun!
You teach me to repeat ˈ the praises you have giv'n:
To glorify – rejoice ˈ *in God, your Saviour-Son.*
Like mystic roses are ˈ your words of love. They go
To make all ages sweet ˈ from what you have professed.
He – the Almighty – *has* ˈ done great things in you! so
I want to think on them ˈ that thus may God be blessed.

8   Saint Joseph didn't know ' what miracle was here.
    A *tabernacle*, you ' had secrets, then, to keep –
    Such Beauty you enclosed! ' (See, Joseph standing near.)
    So humble were you! He, ' not knowing, had to weep.
    Your *silence*, Mary – oh, ' I love its *eloquence*! –
    A gentle harmony ' of sounds that thrill and move.
    It speaks of what is great ' – of the omnipotence
    Of one who simply waits ' for help from up above.

9   O Joseph! Mary! Then ' you went to Bethlehem.
    I see you turned away ' – 'no room' at each inn-gate.
    From all who lived there . . . well, ' what help had you from
                them?
    Poor strangers get 'no room'; ' the place goes to the great.
    The place goes to the great; ' *and yours a stable is –*
    That's where the Queen of Heav'n ' *has to bring God to birth!*
    O Saviour's Mother, you're ' so lovable in this!
    How great I find you, in ' so poor a part of earth.

10 When Love Eternal wrapped ' in swaddling clothes I see,
    And, from the Word of God, ' such little cries I hear,
    Angelic-spirits then ' no envy rouse in me,
    For, look! their Lord and God ' is now my Brother dear.
    You, Mary! – how I bless ' you, who upon these shores
    Have made bud forth and bloom ' that Flower of Heaven
                there!
    Then, with the Shepherds, Kings ' . . . that listening of
                yours:
    You guarded, in your heart, ' *all things with quiet care.*

11 With other women who ' had come there, you're upon
    The Holy Temple mount! ' I love you, as I see
    You lift Him up, and so ' present to Simeon
    The Saviour of our souls ' . . . he holds Him tenderly.

[174]

At first it's with a smile ' I hear the old man sing:
But soon his tones have changed; ' they start me weeping,
    when
What words of future grief ' his prophesyings bring! –
For he presents to you ' a sword of sorrows then.

12 Up to the evening hours ' of life (O Martyrs' Queen!)
This sorrow-bearing sword ' *will pierce you through the
    heart*:
Already – to escape ' from Herod's jealous spleen,
You have to rise and from ' your native soil depart –
As Jesus sleeps in peace, ' wrapped round with your veil-folds,
St Joseph comes and says ' that you must up and fly!
Obedience's *own* ' unveiling one beholds:
You leave – without delay: ' you never question why.

13 Yet, Mary, this I think ' that there in Egypt, and
In poverty! such joy ' you, even then, are giv'n:
For, Jesus – *isn't He* ' *the loveliest Native Land*?
What matters exile, for ' you're still possessing Heav'n?
But in Jerusalem, ' so bitter then . . . distress
Did – vast as might a sea ' flood in – this joy succeed:
Jesus, throughout three days, ' *hid from your tenderness –*
That, for severity, ' an exile was indeed!

14 Then, joy of love – He's found! ' with doctors of the law;
And, to the lovely Child ' who charms them all, one hears:
'O Son, why did you act ' in this way, tell us! Your
Father and I have been ' looking for you in tears!'
And God, a Child, replies ' – how deep the Mystery! –
(Your arms stretched out to him) ' asks of his Mother dear:
'Why was it that you searched ' for me? – did not you see
That I must be about ' my Father's business here?'

15 The Gospel tells me, in ' His wisdom, Jesus crossed
   To Joseph and to you ' 'was subject'. Yes, He stayed
   Submissive, tenderly ' (in awe at this I'm lost).
   My heart says, always His ' dear parents He obeyed.
   And now I understand ' the Temple's Mystery.
   This lovely King – in words, ' in tone of speaking too –   ★³
   This Child of yours desires ' that we *example* see –
   Souls in the night of faith ' should seek Him as did you!

16 Since Heaven's King has willed ' that His own Mother
        should
   Be subject to this night ' such anguish to possess,
   One asks her: 'Here, on earth, ' to suffer, then, is good?'
   'To suffer, *when you love* ' *is purest happiness!*' . . .
   Ah, He can take back all ' that He has given me
   (No need to *ask* me! – tell ' Him that). I do not doubt
   That He can hide, but I'll ' be waiting, you will see! –
   Till all is endless Day ' (faith then a lamp put out).

17 At Nazareth your life ' (O Virgin full of grace!)
   Was poor – you didn't long ' for comforts not possessed:
   Did transports, raptures come ' or miracles? No trace
   Of these bedecked you there, ' O Queen of all the Blest!
   Their number's very great, ' your little ones on earth;
   To lift up fearless eyes ' – this joy to them is giv'n.
   It's by *the common way* ' (O Mother beyond worth!)
   That you are pleased to walk, ' to guide them up to Heav'n.

18 I want to follow you ' each day, my Mother dear –
   To live with you, though I'm ' still exiled from above!
   I plunge into your heart; ' enraptured, I revere,
   O Virgin, seeing there, ' *such an abyss of love!*
   Beneath that mother's-gaze ' I never fear; in turn
   It teaches me to *weep* ' and then *rejoice* with you!

[176]

My days of holy fun ' you're never going to spurn;
You want to share them, and ' you deign to bless them too.

19 At Cana, when you saw ' how worried were that pair
(They couldn't hide it, they ' were running out of wine),
You told your Son, in your ' solicitude and care:
You hoped for answer from ' the Saviour's power divine.
To start with, Jesus some ' resistance seemed to show –
'Woman, with you and me ' what has this thing to do?'.
What did His Heart-deeps say? ' He calls you Mother, so
A miracle – His first – ' He worked there, and for you.

20 One day there was a crowd ' of sinners, being taught
By Him who wanted them ' to come to Heav'n; and when
They said to Jesus you ' were on the hill and sought,
Mother, to speak with Him ' – ah, your Divine Son then
(To demonstrate to us ' His love's immensity),
In front of all the crowd ' upon the hill-side spread:
'Who is my brother, who ' my sister, mother? He
Is that, who does my will', ' Jesus the Saviour said.

21 O Spotless Virgin, my ' most tender Mother, at
The side of Jesus, as ' you listened to Him . . . see,
You – not made sad by this – ' rejoiced He shows us that
Our souls, and here below, ' become *His family*!
Yes, you rejoiced that He ' gives us His own Life here –
The Treasures, infinite, ' of His Divinity . . . .
How could one fail to bless ' you, Mary, hold you dear,
When seeing all that love, ' all that humility?

22 As Jesus loves us, so ' you truly love us, too:
For our sake you consent ' to draw back from Him thus:
For, love is giving all ' is giving self – that you
Desired to prove, as you ' remained supporting us.

And your vast tenderness ' the Saviour's seen. He knows
Your tender Mother's heart, ' its secrets! *He has giv'n*
To sinners, you to be ' *our Refuge: when He rose*
And left His saving Cross, ' *to wait for us in Heav'n.*

23　Mary – beside the Cross ' and like a priest! – I see
You offering to God, ' the Father up above
(Appeasing Justice there), ' on top of Calvary,
Gentle Emmanuel, ' Jesus, your own heart's-love!
A prophet once said this ' (O Mother, stricken so):
'There is no sorrow like ' Your sorrow . . . .' And you would
Stay exiled here! You were, ' for us *unstinting*, O
Queen of the Martyrs! *with* ' *your very heart's life-blood.*

24　Saint John's house then becomes ' your only haven – when
Instead of Jesus you'd ' the son of Zebedee!
That told, the Gospels give ' no further detail then –
About the Virgin they ' speak nothing more to me.　★4
But, silence so profound ' . . . my Mother, does not this
Suggest *the Word would wish,* ' *Himself, to manifest*
The secrets of your life ' ah, what a song is His
Eternally to charm ' your *children*, Heaven's Blest!

25　This gentle music I ' shall hear soon, and arrive
In Heav'n, to see you . . . you ' came down to see
me – how
You smiled upon me in ' the morning of my life!
Still, Mother, smile on me! ' for it is evening now.
No longer do I fear ' your blaze of splendour: I
Have suffered with you. This ' I am preparing for:
To sing, upon your knee, ' 'I love you – listen why';
'O Mary! I'm your child' ' I'll sing for evermore!

Notes

PN 54

May 1897

'Do not be afraid of loving the Blessed Virgin *too much*, you will *never* love her enough, and Jesus will be very happy, because the Blessed Virgin is His Mother' (Thérèse, letter of 30 May 1889 to Marie Guérin).

'We oughtn't to say unlikely things, or what we don't know anything about: for example, that when she was very little, at the age of three, the Blessed Virgin went to the Temple to offer herself to God with quite extraordinary feelings of burning love; whereas perhaps she went there very simply to obey her parents' (*Last Conversations*, 21 August 1897).

Mary 'is more Mother than Queen', said Thérèse. This is much quoted. But, by contrast with some today who seemingly cannot overstress the 'ordinariness' of her who bore God Incarnate, Thérèse (who was reacting to an opposite exaggeration, for example, the writer who in 1842 said that the angels and all the blessed, when they see Our Lady, 'hide themselves for shame' as the stars are eclipsed by the sun) was balanced in her expression. 'It is good to speak of (Our Lady's) prerogatives,' she said; rightly adding that 'one should not stop at this' (*il ne faut pas dire que cela*), otherwise people might 'feel a certain estrangement' from someone presented as so lofty and unapproachable.

The Mother of Our Redeemer (though wholly a creature, and redeemed like us, albeit in anticipation of her conceiving and mothering Christ) *is*, as it were, a blaze of light (stanza 1, *ta sublime gloire*): but Thérèse – who knows that Mary is our tender mother also – is not dazzled. Pius XII's Marian Year prayer to Our Lady stresses both facets when it begins: 'Enraptured by the splendour of your heavenly beauty, and impelled by the anxieties of the world, we cast ourselves into your arms, O Immaculate Mother of Jesus and our Mother . . .'

Italics In the French, Thérèse italicizes much, to stress important points. These italics have been followed in the translation. (However, the *small* italicizations in stanzas 1, 2, 4, 5, 7, 12, 15 and 16 follow Thérèse's general sense rather than any italicization of her own.)

St. 16, l. 6 'No need to ask me'. Thérèse uses a phrase which means 'Don't stand on ceremony with me'.

St. 23, l. 4 To the present translator Thérèse's words brought to mind a moving phrase by Alfred Noyes which refers to the period between the Annunciation and the Birth of Christ: '. . . her whose life-blood once had throbbed in Him'.

St. 23, ll. 7–8 In a letter to the Abbé Bellière (December 1896) Thérèse wrote of 'martyrdom of the heart'.

St. 25, l. 3 'You smiled upon me': a reference to her cure, in 1883, at Les Buissonnets, when a statue of the Virgin appeared to smile at her, penetrating 'to the very depths of my soul' (Ms. A).

★¹ Here (and in Stanzas 16, 20 and 22) Th addressed Mary by name, as in Stanzas 1 and 25. Elsewhere she used adjectives of endearment in addressing her heavenly Mother.

★² 'on your knee' is P's. Th wrote '*ravie*', 'in delight'. The setting, in both versions, is that of Mary's visitation to her cousin Elisabeth; the 'sacred song' the Magnificat.

★³ 'in words, in tone of speaking' (*La réponse, le ton*) is P's.

★⁴ P, 'Virgin'; Th, 'Queen of Heaven'.

[50]

YOU, KNOWING I'M AS
SMALL AS I CAN BE

You, knowing I'm as small as I can be,
Are glad in stooping down, *You* little too:
White Sacrament I love! Oh come to me,
Come to me, for my heart aspires to You! –
And (after such a favour) grant that I
May die of love – I beg You – and depart . . .
Hear, Jesus, as in tenderness I cry:
     'Come to my heart!'

Notes

PS 8

July 1897

Thérèse wrote this poem on the night of 12–13 July.

Before her Holy Communion, in the infirmary on the morning of 16 July, Feast of Our Lady of Mount Carmel, Sr Marie of the Eucharist (Marie Guérin) sang these lines for her in a 'high and beautiful' voice: and, after Communion, sang for her Stanza 14 of her poem '*Vivre d'Amour*' (Poem 17): 'Dying of Love . . . so sweet a martyrdom . . .'

INDEX OF TITLES

	Poem
Angel of the Desert, The	25
Aviary of the Child Jesus, The	39
Comment on the Divine	29
Divine Dew, The, or The Virginal Milk of Mary	1
Divine Little Beggar-boy of Christmas, The	24
Eternal Hymn, sung from exile, The	28
Hymn of Saint Agnes	26
Hymn to obtain the canonization of the Venerable Joan of Arc	4
Hymn to the Holy Face	19
I thirst for love!	30
Jesus, my Love, recall!	22
Jesus Only	35
Joan at Domrémy	2
Joan in Heaven: the Canticle of Triumph	14
Joan's Hymn after her Victories	10
Joan's Prayer in Prison	11
Joan's Voices during her Martyrdom	12
Joan: the Divine Judgment	13
Lily in the midst of thorns, A	48
Living by Love!	17
Melody of Saint Cecilia, The	3
My Arms	44
My Heaven, there for me!	31
My Hope	32
My Peace and my Joy!	41
My Longings before the Tabernacle	23
My Song of Today	5
Prayer of France to Joan of Arc	15
Prayer of the Child of a Saint	6
Queen of Heaven, to her well-loved child, Marie, The	8

Sacristans of Carmel, The   36
Song of Thanks of Jesus's Betrothed   16
Still a Song of Love   37
Story of a Shepherdess become Queen, The   7
Surrender's the Delicious Fruit of Love   47
Sweet Remembrance   27
Throwing of Flowers   33
To my Guardian Angel   42
To my Little Brothers in Heaven, the Holy Innocents   40
To Our Lady of Perpetual Succour   45
To Our Lady of Victories   34
To Saint Joseph   9
To the Child Jesus   38
To the Sacred Heart   21
To the Venerable Théophane Vénard   43
Un-petaled Rose, An   46
What I loved . . . (The Canticle of Céline)   18
Why I love you, Mary!   49
You have broken my bonds, O Lord!   20
You, knowing I'm as small as I can be   50

INDEX OF FIRST LINES

	Poem
Ah, Jesus! my name you know	38
A little child I'm seeking, who's	8
All, all! to You, Almighty, be	10
Each evening, what a joy when votive-flowers are thrown	33
First, Jesus, Mary's hands made sure you didn't fall	46
For exiles here, His love to show	39
For love of You, my God! for that alone I go	2
From the Almighty I have taken arms	44
From the Eternal Country we come down	12
Glorious Guardian of my soul	42
Happiness – people search for it	41
I hear your voice on high – I answer you, my love	13
I sing the Holy Family! they are	25
Jesus, my God, I'm praying now to tell	37
Jesus (your Treasure and your own!)	24
List'ning in Love's hushed Evening, you'd have heard	17
Lord, You have chosen me and since my childhood days	48
My gentle Jesus, on Your Mother's breast	1
My heart – it needs to prove its tenderness	35
My life's a jot of time, an hour that comes and goes	5
My Love is Christ: He is my very life, and He	26
My Voices told of this: in prison I am thrown	11
No job we do could be as nice	36
Now all the Blest in Heav'n sing out your praise	43
O God of Hosts, the Church – the whole of us	4
O happy key, since you exist	23
O happy Little Ones! – ah, with what tenderness	40
Oh, how I love the memory	18
O Jesus! it's today you break my bonds, and I	20
O Mary, I would sing '*I love you – this is why*'	49

O Saint I love so much, with joy I contemplate   3
Recall how from Your Father's glory You   22
Recall that here on earth your happiness   6
Remember, Joan, the country of your birth   15
Seeking her Jesus, to the Sepulchre   21
Since I was young, of course, your picture here   45
There is on earth a Tree   47
The world (to my great happiness)   29
This crown is yours, and for eternity   14
Though I am still upon this foreign shore   32
Though poverty of life you knew   9
To bear with exile, in this vale of tears, I need   31
To you, my Mother – who obtain   34
We've come to sing, O Madeleine   7
What could I ever compare   27
You, Jesus – God – an exile here below   30
You, knowing I'm as small as I can be   50
Your bride who's exiled here upon this foreign shore   28
Your picture, Jesus, like a star   19
You've hidden me, O Jesus, in Your Face   16

NOTES TO TRANSLATOR'S
INTRODUCTION

———

Abbreviations

Aut. Thérèse's autobiography, *Story of a Soul* (comprising Manuscripts A, B and C). The quoted extracts are translated by me; but references are given to the following complete translations of the autobiography: *Autobiography of a Saint*, tr. Ronald Knox (London: HarperCollins Publishers, Fount Classics) and *Story of a Soul*, tr. John Clarke, O.C.D. (Washington, D.C.: ICS Publications, second ed., 1976).

LC *Thérèse of Lisieux: her last conversations*, tr. John Clarke, O.C.D. (ICS Publications, 1977). References are to the Yellow Notebook (*Carnet Jaune*) unless otherwise indicated.

LT Indicates Thérèse's own letters in *Letters of St Thérèse of Lisieux*, 2 vols., tr. John Clarke, O.C.D. (ICS Publications, 1982). References are also given to *Collected Letters of Saint Thérèse of Lisieux*, ed. Abbé Combes, tr. F. J. Sheed (London: Sheed & Ward, 1949).

M *A memoir of my sister St Thérèse by Sister Geneviève of the Holy Face* (Céline), tr. The Carmelite Sisters of New York (Dublin: M. H. Gill and Son Ltd, 1959), Céline's '*Conseils et Souvenirs*' including reminiscences by other former novices of Thérèse formed a chapter in later editions of *Histoire d'une Ame*; some of these reminiscences were used in depositions to the Canonical Process of Beatification and Canonization.

'Deposition' in these notes refers to testimony to one or both of the tribunals in the Canonical Process, the Diocesan (1910–11) and the Apostolic (1915–16), pub. Teresianum, Rome.

O' M *St Thérèse of Lisieux by those who knew her*, ed. and tr. Christopher O'Mahoney (Dublin: Veritas Publications, 1975). This contains translations of depositions by fifteen witnesses to the tribunal of 1910–11.

1 John 14:15

2 'I cannot explain this [her physical suffering] except by the ardent desires I have had to save souls' (Thérèse, on the day of her death): LC, 205

3 Poem 50.

4 1 John 4:19

5 Poem 35, St. 5

6 Poem 27, St. 2

7 Poem 38, St. 3

8 Poem 17, St. 3

9 Deposition of Sr Marthe de Jésus, 1911 (O'M, 227).

10 Poem 11, St. 4 ('pour m'unir à Jésus')

11 *The Eagle and the Dove* (London: Sphere Books Ltd.): St Thérèse of Lisieux, x.

12 Poem 18, St. 10

13 Poem 22, St. 19

14 Poem 26, St. 3

15 Poem 27, St. 3

16 Songs of Songs, 8:5 ('Under the apple tree I raised thee up'.)

17 *Spiritual Canticle*, XXIII, 2; italics mine.

18 Sermon 32 on the Songs of Songs, from *St Bernard's Sermons*, tr. Backhouse (London: Hodder & Stoughton).

19 *Aut.* (Ms. A); Knox, 54–55 (Ch. VII); Clarke, 45.

20 1 Corinthians 2:9

21 1 John 3:2

22 Quoted by Bl. Elizabeth of the Trinity, *Heaven in Faith*, 23. A German theologian has the striking phrase, a 'belonging to one another mutually of God and the creature' in heaven.

23 Introduction to Bruno, *St John of the Cross* (London: Sheed & Ward, 1932)

24 Letter, 27–29 July 1890; LT 109; Sheed, LXXXVII

25 Poem 22, St. 6

26 Poem 17, St. 1

27 Poem 3, lines 63–64

28 Deposition of Sr Marie of the Trinity, 1916 (and 1911, O'M, 235; slightly different wording).

29 Poem 17, St. 14. The frequency with which Thérèse in her poems uses the metaphor of fire is remarkable.

30 Poem 46, St. 2

31 Poem 21, St. 6

32 Poem 29, St. 3.

33 Poem 36, St. 6

34 Poem 18, St. 50

35 Thérèse's Act of Offering to Merciful Love, 9 June 1895; *Aut.*, Clarke, 276–7. Céline speaks of Thérèse's 'voluntary participation in the Passion of Christ . . . foreseen in her Act of Oblation [Act of Offering] according to the degree willed by Our Lord', M, 83.

36 Blosius (Louis de Blois), *Comfort for the Faint-hearted*, Ch. XXIX; his heading to a quotation from Tauler.

37 Poem 49, St. 5

38 Letter to her sister, Pauline (Sr Agnès de Jésus, later Mère Agnès), 3 September 1890; LT 114; Sheed, LXXXIX

39 LC (7 August 1897), 140. By an error of transcription, no doubt, the Clarke translation omits 'without offending the good God' ('*sans offenser le bon Dieu*').

40 Poem 17, St. 6

41 Poem 21, St. 4

42 Poem 29, St. 3

43 LC (25 July 1897 – Marie), 239

44 *Aut.* (Ms. C); Knox, 224 (Ch. XXXVI); Clarke, 238.

45 Poem 21, St. 7

46 *Aut.* (Ms. C); Knox, 194–5 (Ch. XXXI); Clarke, 207–8. Thérèse did not attribute to herself the virtues she practised.

47 2 Corinthians 12:9 (God's power 'is made perfect in infirmity', *ibid.*)

48 Newman's hymn, 'Firmly I believe and truly.'

49 St Teresa of Avila (*Interior Castle*, VI Mansions, X) describes humility as 'walking in the truth'.

50 '. . . make haste and come down . . .' (Luke, 19:5); LT 137, Sheed, CXVI; M, 28

51 John 3:30

52 Memoir in *Conseils et Souvenirs*

53 The Jerusalem Bible (London: Darton, Longman & Todd).

54 Letter to Céline, 15 October 1889; LT 96, Sheed LXXIV

55 Letter to Céline, 19 October 1892; LT 137; Sheed, CXVI

56 Poem 37, St. 2

57 Algar Thorold, *Catholic Mysticism*, 1900, pp. 125 and 145; italics mine.

58 *Novissima Verba*, 17 July 1897; LC (Additional Conversations, July 1897), 257; depositions of Mère Agnès (Pauline), 1910 (O'M, 21) and 1915.

59 Memoir in *Conseils et Souvenirs*.

60 Act of Offering, *op. cit.*; LC (23 June 1897), 67

61 Deposition of Sr Geneviève (Céline), 1910 (O'M, 125).

62 *Aut.* (Ms. C); Knox, 228 (Ch. XXXVII); Clarke, 242.

63 *Aut.* (Ms. A); Knox, 160 (Ch. XXVI); Clarke, 165.

64 *Aut.* (Ms. A); Knox, 175–6 (Ch. XXIX); Clarke, 180.

65 Poem 47, St. 6

66 Poem 22, St. 20

67 Isaiah 66:12; *Aut.* (Ms. C), Knox, 195 (Ch. XXXI); Clarke, 208.

68 Poem 39, St. 8

69 Poem 17, St. 6

70 Thérèse herself said to Sr Marie of the Trinity: '. . . be very careful in explaining it, for our "little way", badly understood, could be taken for quietism or illuminism.'

71 R. P. Victor de la Vièrge, O.C.D. (Victor Sion), *Spiritual Realism of St Thérèse of Lisieux* (Thomas More Books Ltd, 1962), 34; a masterly book on Thérèse's spirituality.

72 Poem 7, St. 5

73 One speaks figuratively, of course: 'I never see her run,' the gardener said, of her religious bearing in actuality: deposition of Sr Marie of the Angels, 1911 (O'M, 211). Thérèse's own '*run*, not *rest*' (M, 57) was a metaphor.

74 Deposition of Mère Agnès, 1910 (O'M, 44).

75 Poem 21, St. 4

76 Guy Gaucher, *The Spiritual Journey of St Thérèse of Lisieux*, London: Darton, Longman & Todd (U.S., *The Story of a Life*, San Francisco: HarperCollins*Publishers*, 1987), Part III, 5.

77 Poem 17, St. 5

78 Poem 35, St. 5

79 Poem 44, St. 1

80 *Ibid.*, St. 5

81 Mid-*word*, indeed: deposition of Sr Marie of the Sacred Heart (Thérèse's sister, Marie), 1910 (O'M, 100). '. . . the pen or the needle was put aside instantly': M, 151

82 e.g. *Aut.* (Ms. C); Knox, 211–12 (Ch. XXXIV); Clarke, 222–3.

83 *Aut.* (Ms. A); Knox, 106 (Ch. XVI); Clarke, 102.

84 Deposition of Sr Marie of the Trinity, 1911 (O'M, 235). The French here translated 'insignificant' is '*indifférents*'.

85 Memoir in *Conseils et Souvenirs*. 'Nothing sticks to my hands, everything I have, everything I gain, is for the Church and souls': Thérèse, depositions of Mère Agnès, 1910 (O'M, 50) and 1915; LC (12 July 1897), 91.

86 Letter to Céline, 6 July 1893; LT 142; Sheed, CXXI

87 Depositions of Sr Marie of the Trinity, 1911 (O'M, 234) and 1916. On hearing that an author had 'failed in respect and submission to a bishop,' Thérèse stopped reading his books and 'never wished to hear them spoken of again': *The Spirit of St Thérèse de L'Enfant Jesus* (Burns Oates & Washbourne Ltd., 1925), 67.

88 Poem 22, St. 17

89 *Ibid.*, St. 16

90 *Ibid.*, St. 25

91 Poem 5, St. 10

92 *Aut.* (Ms. A); Knox, 103 (Ch. XV); Clarke, 99.

93 *Aut.* (Ms. A); Knox, 104 (Ch. XV); Clarke, 101.

94 *Aut.* (Ms. C); Knox, 202 (Ch. XXXII); Clarke, 214.

95 Poem 22, St. 27 (see translation note underneath poem)

96 'It is so sweet to serve the good God in the night of trial . . .', *Conseils et Souvenirs*; M, 197.

97 *Aut.* (Ms. C), *op. cit.*, note 94.

98 LC (28 August 1897), 173

99 LC (24 September 1897), 199

100 Letters to Céline, 12 March and 4 April 1889; LT 85 and 87; Sheed, LXI and LXIII

101 Letter of 4 April, *op. cit.*

102 Letter to Céline, Christmas 1896; LT 211; Sheed, CLXXXII

103 *Aut.* (Ms. A); Knox, 82 (Ch. XII); Clarke, 77.

104 Guy Gaucher, *The Passion of St Thérèse of Lisieux*, tr. by Sr Anne Marie Brennan, OCD, pub., St Paul Publications 1989.

105 An earlier record (*Novissima Verba*) has: '. . . never asked the good God for suffering.' See also LC, 290 (letter of Sr Marie of the Eucharist – Marie Guérin – to her father, 27 August 1897).

106 LC (26 August 1897), 169.

107 LC (11 August 1897), 145

108 Poem 34, St. 4

109 Poem 23, St. 7

110 Poem 16, St. 2

111 *Aut.* (Ms. A); Knox, 148 (Ch. XXIV); Clarke, 149.

112 Poem 30, Refrain 2

113 Poem 41, St. 5

114 Sr Marthe reports Thérèse as having said once: '. . . what a joy it is to suffer for someone you love!' (deposition, 1911, O'M, 219); and see Poem 49, St. 16.

115 e.g. 175 (30 August 1897); 184 (5 September 1897)

116 *Spiritual Canticle*, IX, 6

117 LC (13 July 1897), 95

118 Poem 17, St. 9

119 Song of Songs, 2:10–12

120 LC (4 July 1897), 73

121 LC (30 September 1897), 205; deposition of Mère Agnès, 1910 (O'M, 68).

122 LC (30 September 1897), 206. LC, Céline, 230, and also Pauline's (Mère Agnès's) deposition, 1915, have 'I wouldn't want to suffer less!'

123 LC (30 September 1897), 206; depositions of Mère Agnès, 1910 (O'M, 69) and 1915.

124 Poem 8, St. 18

125 LC, 102; see also LT 254; Sheed, CCXXV.

126 Hans Urs von Balthasar, *Thérèse of Lisieux*, tr. Donald Nicholl (London: Sheed & Ward, 1953), 31; later edition, *Two Sisters in the Spirit: Thérèse of Lisieux and Elizabeth of the Trinity* (San Francisco: Ignatius Press, 1992), 74–75. I have been greatly indebted to that book in the writing of the present Introduction (though I dare to be in less than total sympathy with just a few of its conclusions).

127 e.g. deposition of Sr Marie of the Trinity, 1911 (O'M, 230).

128 Of the writers in English who have noticed the poems, some have summarily dismissed them. Even the admirable John Beevers (*Saint Thérèse, the Little Flower*, Rockford, Illinois, Tan Books and Publishers Inc., 1976, Ch. 5) says that they are 'quite without distinction'. Frances Parkinson Keyes (*Written in Heaven*, Dublin: Clonmore & Reynolds Ltd., 1946, Ch. IX) praises their 'rhythmic quality', 'fluency' and 'grace'.

129 At least in relation to the autobiography: 'I haven't had time to write

what I wished, it isn't complete. But listen, Mother: anything that you will find it good to cut out or to add to the notebook of my life [*Novissima Verba* has 'add what I have said to you by word of mouth'], it is (as though) I am cutting it out and adding it. Remember that later and have no scruple, no doubt, on this subject': Thérèse, July 1897, *Cahiers Verts*.

130 For example, Pauline retouched Poem 17, stanza 1, to make it include the image of the loving and obedient soul as a *palace*, a living abode for the Father and the Son. Thérèse had used the same image in her play *The Little Beggar-boy of Christmas*, the heart as a palace for the Christ Child, born in a stable.

131 An exception is Poem 49, where I follow Thérèse's italicization closely.

Catechism of the Catholic Church, quoted in Foreword and Translator's Introduction, is published by Geoffrey Chapman, London, 1994.

John Beevers' translation of St Thérèse's autobiography (introduction quoted on page 157) is published by Image Books, Doubleday, New York, 1989.

The quotation from Sr Teresa Margaret, D.C., on page 107, is from *I Choose All* (Fowler Wright Books Ltd., Tenbury Wells, 1964).

The quotation from Alfred Noyes on page 180 is from the poem *The Assumption* in *A Letter to Lucian and other Poems* (London: John Murray, 1956).